Leadership
Can Be Child's Play

Suresh Srinivasan

77 simple & implementable leadership lessons
from the most ancient contemporary management book,
Srimad Bhagavad Geetaa

...leadership simplified

BLUEROSE PUBLISHERS
India | U.K.

Copyright © Suresh Srinivasan 2025

All rights reserved by author. No part of this publication may be reproduced, stored in a retrieval system or transmitted in any form or by any means, electronic, mechanical, photocopying, recording or otherwise, without the prior permission of the author. Although every precaution has been taken to verify the accuracy of the information contained herein, the publisher assumes no responsibility for any errors or omissions. No liability is assumed for damages that may result from the use of information contained within.

BlueRose Publishers takes no responsibility for any damages, losses, or liabilities that may arise from the use or misuse of the information, products, or services provided in this publication.

For permissions requests or inquiries regarding this publication, please contact:

BLUEROSE PUBLISHERS
www.BlueRoseONE.com
info@bluerosepublishers.com
+91 8882 898 898
+4407342408967

ISBN: 978-93-7018-089-5

Cover design: Yash Singhal
Typesetting: Namrata Saini

First Edition: May 2025

Book In Memory
Of
My Father

Late Shri C S Srinivasan
1930 to 2019

Leadership
Can Be Child's Play

One leadership lesson every day to contemplate upon, & 77 days which can transform your professional life…
…and maybe your colleagues around you

*To my dear friends: Devi Prasad Choudhury,
Rear Admiral KC Sekhar (Retd.), Ravi Kumar Seshan,
Srikant Sree Ram.*

*And to my wife, Radha, my best friend, who made all of my
dreams possible. Where would I be without you?*

Preface

Imagine if leadership could be as effortless as a child's play. No struggle, no stress, just a joyful expression of our true selves.

The Bhagavad Geetaa, ancient India's timeless wisdom text, reveals that such leadership is not only possible but also essential. Through its profound teachings, we discover that leadership is not about power, position, or authority, but about embracing our innate curiosity, creativity, and sense of wonder.

In the Geetaa, we find the inspiring story of Arjunaa, a warrior-prince who embodies the struggles and triumphs of modern leaders. As he navigates the complexities of duty, desire, and self-discovery, we learn valuable lessons about the nature of leadership, identity, and purpose.

This book invites you to embark on a transformative journey, exploring the Geetaa's wisdom and unlocking the secrets of effortless leadership.

Join me on this exciting adventure, as we uncover the hidden treasures of the Bhagavad Geetaa and unlock the full potential of leadership as child's play.

This book is divided into three sections – Knowledge, Attitude, and Skill.

Suresh Srinivasan
Chief Enthusiasm Officer

Foreword

"Get up and set your shoulder to the wheel, how long is this life for? As you have come into this world leave some mark behind."

In this miraculous world, we find divine souls treading the path along with us who leave a distinct impression on our minds. Lives of such persons are worth emulating as they live the saying- **"You can either be an example or a warning." The choice is yours**.

Bhagavad Geetaa can be stated to be the foremost amongst the works that can transform the life of a person.

In this ever changing world there are few people who lead the aggressive good way and give the world direction to do something and leave the world a better place than they found it. One such person is Suresh Srinivasan who has impressed me from the time he came to my office with this late divine father Shri C.S.Srinivasan.

The book written by Suresh gives one more angle to the bliss giving Bhagavad Geetaa in as much as the 77 slokas are explained in simple and enchanting manner.

It has been a pleasure to go through the facets of knowledge, attitude and skill as explained in the book which is lucid and easy to understand.

I wish the readers a great journey in their lives which I am sure will show a distinct improvement, should the lessons of the book get ingrained in the personality.

May the lord Krishnaa bless us all.

J S Kini
Advocate High Court, Bombay

The Backdrop

In the battlefield at Kurukshetra, Arjunaa tells Krishnaa, the charioteer, to take the chariot between both armies, which Krishnaa does. As Arjunaa surveys the enemy lines at Kurukshetra, he's confronted with a distressing sight: his own relatives, friends, and mentors, including his grandfather Bheeshma and his guru Dronaa, are arrayed against him.

Arjunaa is overcome with emotion and moral anguish. He's torn between his duty as a warrior (swadharmaa) and his personal relationships with those on the opposing side.

Arjunaa's Despondency

In Chapter 1 of the Bhagavad Geetaa, Arjunaa confesses to Krishnaa:

"My limbs fail, my mouth is parched, my body trembles... I see evil omens, O Krishnaa... I do not wish to kill them, even if it means winning the three worlds."

Arjunaa's emotional turmoil is so intense that he's unable to hold his bow, Gaandiva. He's paralyzed by his conflicting emotions and moral doubts.

Krishnaa's Advice

Krishnaa, Arjunaa's charioteer and spiritual guide, observes Arjunaa's distress and begins to offer his advice. Krishnaa's words of wisdom will form the core of the Bhagavad Geetaa's teachings on dharma, duty, leadership, and spiritual growth.

Krishnaa's advice will help Arjunaa navigate his moral dilemma, reconcile his conflicting emotions, and ultimately find the courage to fulfil his duty as a warrior.

A Note to the Hesitant Reader

When I say, "*Leadership can be Child's Play,* people either tell me that Leadership is not easy or that following core leadership principles on the job is unrealistic. However when I say "child's play", what I mean is, "the way a child plays" rather than easy, as commonly thought of. Let's take a step back and think of how children play:

1) Children play with curiosity - they follow their interests and ask questions.
2) They are not afraid to try things. They may build things that break or fall while building them, but that doesn't stop them from trying something new.
3) Children invent stories, characters, and solutions to imaginary problems.
4) Children are perceptive of their loved ones' feelings. They may test their boundaries with elders, but they learn empathy in a group setting, which is a foundation of emotional intelligence.
5) Last and most importantly, children rarely care about finishing things perfectly. They are in it for the experience. They are in it for the process and not the product.

There are many ways to be a leader, but fewer ways to be a great one. Thinking of leadership as child's play can be one of them….

Benefits of Implementing These 77 Leadership Lessons

Sanjayaa, in the following shlokaa, says that he is convinced that fortune, victory, power, and virtues will all come to the one who applies these learnings.

18.78 **Yatra Yogesh Varak Krishna Ha
Yatra Paartho Dhanur Dhara Ha
Tatra Shrir Vijayo Bhooti Hi
Dhruvaa Neetir Matir Mama**

Wherever there is the Supreme Lord Krishnaa, the master of those following the science of uniting the individual consciousness (wave, bubble, froth) with the Ultimate consciousness (ocean), and where there is Arjunaa; there is firmly established, Unending Opulence, Victory, Prosperity, and Righteousness. This is my resolve.

The benefits of implementing these leadership lessons are that one will gain clarity of thought, a bias for the right action, a positive attitude, the achievement of organizational goals, and ability to lead a happy, peaceful, and stress-free life, resulting in abundance.

Section 1
Knowledge

Live as if you were to die tomorrow.
Learn as if you were to live forever –
  Mahatma Gandhi

Leadership Shlokaas: - 1

Arjunaa, in the following shlokaas, is asking Krishnaa to take the chariot between the two armies to find out who are all fighting from Duryodhanaa's side so that he could understand the problem context, thereby plan his strategy accordingly.

1:20   Atha Vyavas Thitaan Dhris Tvaa
       Dhaarta Raash Traan Kapid Dhvaja Ha
       Pra Vrittey Shastra Sam Paatey
       Dhanur Udyamya Paandava Ha

Then, Arjunaa, seeing Dhritaraashtraa's soldiers standing arrayed and ready to discharge their weapons, Arjunaa – the son of Paandu, who had monkey on his flag, took up his bow and…

1:21   Hrishi Keshan Tadaa Vaakyam
       Ida Maaha Mahee Patey
       Arjunaa Uvaa Cha
       Senayor Ubhayor Madhyey
       Ratham Sthaa Paya Mey Chyuta

1:22   Yaava Detaan Nireek Sheham
       Yoddhu Kaamaa Na Vasthi Taan
       Kair Mayaa Saha Yod Dhavyam
       Asmin Rana Samudya Mey

…said the following words to Krishnaa (Hrishikesha), O Lord of the earth.
Arjunaa said:
Achyuta, please place my chariot between both the armies so that I can look upon those warriors arrayed for battle with whom I must fight.

Additional shlokaas for this leadership lesson in annexure

Leadership Lesson

Do your homework, like market research, competitor analysis, resource assessment, capabilities evaluation, etc., before starting any new project, taking up any new assignment, or assigning new work to your team members.

Leadership Shlokaas: - 2

Krishnaa, in the following shlokaas, tells Arjunaa to see his universal form & shows his "Vishwaroopam – Cosmic form," followed by Sanjayaa telling Dhritaraashtra what he sees on the battlefield.

11:5   Sri Bhagavaan Uvaa Cha
       Pashya Mey Paartha Roopaani
       Shata Shotha Sahas Rasha Ha
       Naa Naa Vidhaani Divyaani
       Naa Naa Varnaa Kriteeni Cha

       Lord Krishnaa said: O Arjunaa, behold My divine, transcendental forms with hundreds and thousands of varieagated types and varieagated colors and forms.

11:6   Pashyaa Dityaan Vasoon Rudraan
       Ash Vinau Marutas Tathaa
       Bahoon Ya Dhrista Poorvaani
       Pashyaa Char Yaani Bhaarata

       Behold the Adityaas, the Vasus, the Rudraas, the Ashwins, and the Maruts; behold the many wonders never seen before, O Bharataa.

11:7   Ihai Kasthan Jagat Kritsnam
       Pashyaad Yasa Charaa Charam
       Mama Dehey Gudaa Kesha
       Yach Chaan Yad Drashtu Micchasi

       Now behold, O Gudaakesha, in this Body, that the whole universe centers in One – including, the moving and the unmoving – and whatever else you desire to see.

Additional shlokaas for this leadership lesson in annexure

Leadership Lesson

Show your team members the BIG picture. Hold a town hall or a meeting with all employees or team members to share the organization's growth plans, the number of branches worldwide, the employee count, etc. This will give your team confidence that they are in the right place, their jobs are secure, reducing attrition and building motivation.

Leadership Shlokaa 3

Krishnaa, in the following shlokaa, tells Arjunaa what type of diet is best for keeping the mind sharp and the body fit & agile most of the time.

17.8   Aayus Sattva Balaa Rogya
Sukha Preeti Vivardha Naa Haa
Rasyaas Snigdhaa Sthiraa Hrid Yaahaa
Aa Haaraas Saat Tvika Priyaa Haa

The foods which increases life, purity, strength, health, joy, and cheerfulness, which are salty, oily, juicy, substantial, and agreeable, are dear to the Sattvic.

Leadership Lesson

Eat the right type of diet to stay mentally and physically fit most of the time. Sattvic foods are believed to increase energy, happiness, calmness, and mental clarity. In practice, this means eating vegetarian, nutritious, fresh, and flavourful foods.

Leadership Shlokaa 4

Krishnaa, in the following shlokaa, tells Arjunaa to keep his senses under control to ensure he makes the right decision.

16.1   Sri Bhagavaan Uvaa Cha
        Abhayam Sat Tvasam Shuddhi Hi
        Nyaana Yoga Vyavas Thiti Hi
        Daanan Damash Cha Yagnyas Cha
        Svaadh Yaayas Tapa Aar Javam

The blessed Lord said:
Fearlessness, purity of heart, established in the wisdom of discrimination of spirit and matter by the science of uniting the individual consciousness with the Ultimate consciousness, charity, **Control of the Senses**, *sacrifice, austerity, and alginment…*

Leadership Lesson

Seek approval from the intellect before making any decision; don't take decisions based on
what the heart tells.
The heart reacts, while the intellect responds. The heart focuses on greed, while the intellect focuses on need.

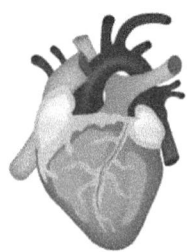 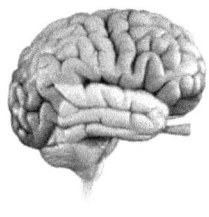

Leadership Shlokaas 5

Krishnaa, in the following shlokaas, tells Arjunaa the do's and don'ts based on the Vedaas, because the intricacies of actions are very mysterious and need to be taught. Krishnaa also advises Arjunaa to keep practicing.

4:17   Karmano Hyapi Bod Dhav Yam
       Bod Dhav Vyancha Vikar Manaha
       Akarma Nascha Bod Dhav Yam
       Gahanaa Karmano Gati Hee

The subject of actions prescribed in the Vedaas should be understood, the subject of actions prohibited in the Vedaas should also be understood. The subject of renunciation of action as prescribed by the Vedaas should be understood, because the intricacies of actions are very mysterious.

12:9   Atha Chittam Samaa Dhaatum
       Nashak Noshi Mayi Sthiram
       Abyaasa Yogena Tata Ha
       Maami Chaaptun Dhanan Jaya

If you are unable to fix your mind steadily on Me, then by constant practice, seek to reach Me, O Dhananjayaa.

Leadership Lesson

Ensure your team members go through regular, implementable training programs for their self-development to make it easy for them to achieve the organization's goal.

Leadership Shlokaa 6

Krishnaa, in the following shlokaa, tells Arjunaa not to disclose these secrets to those who are not interested in spiritual advancement.

18.67 **Idantey Naata Pas Kaaya**
Naa Bhak Taaya Kadaa Chana
Nachaa Shushroo Shavey Vaachyam
Nacha Maam Yobhya Sooyati

You should never disclose this science to one devoid of austerities, nor to one who is not devoted, nor to one adverse to spiritual advancement, and never to anyone who is envious of Me.

Leadership Lesson

Ask your team members whether they are interested in career advancement, growth, or achieving organizational goals, etc. If they say "yes," train them on these leadership principles. Otherwise, keep this knowledge to yourself.

Section 2
Attitude

Be so happy that, when other people look at you, they become happy too.

— Harbhajan Singh Yogi

Leadership Shlokaa 7

Krishnaa, in the following shlokaa, tells Arjunaa to align his thoughts and actions to achieve the desired result.

16.1 Sri Bhagavaan Uvaa Cha
Abhayam Sat Tvasam Shuddhi Hi
Nyaana Yoga Vyavas Thiti Hi
Daanan Damash Cha Yagnyas Cha
Svaadh Yaayas Tapa Aar Javam

The blessed Lord said:
Fearlessness, purity of heart, established in the wisdom of discrimination of spirit and matter by the science of uniting the individual consciousness with the Ultimate consciousness, charity, control of the senses, sacrifice, austerity (strictness), and **Alginment...**

Leadership Lesson

Get to know each team member personally and understand their goals. Then show them how achieving the organizational goals will also help them achieve their personal goals.
Once both are aligned, attrition will decrease, and performance will improve.

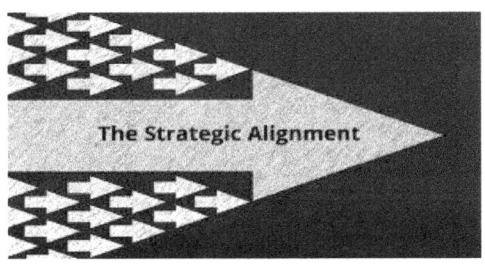

Leadership Shloka-8

Krishnaa, in the following, tells Arjunaa that it is a win-win situation, and he has nothing to lose but only gain.

2:37 **Hatovaa Praap Syasi Svargam**
     Jitvaa Vaa Bhok Shyasey Maheem
     Tasmaad Ut Thishta Kaunteya
     Yud Dhaaya Krita Nischaya Ha

> *If you die, you will attain heavenly worlds, and by gaining victory, you will enjoy earth; therefore, Arjunaa, either way you benefit, so get up and fight.*

Leadership Lesson

Tell your team members that by putting in their 100% effort while doing their tasks, only two things can happen: either they will achieve the goal or learn from the experience. It is a win-win situation for them.

Leadership Shlokaas-9

Krishnaa, in the following shlokaas, tells Arjunaa that if he does not perform his duty as a Kshatriya, he will face the specific negative consequences which will keep his mind agitated for the rest of his life.

2:33 Atha Chetva Mimam Dharmyam
Sam Graaman Na Karish Yasi
Tatas Sva Dharmang Keertim Cha
Hitvaa Paapa Mavaap Syasi

But, if you will not fight this righteous war, having abandoned your own duty, you shall incur sin.

2:34 Akeer Ting Chaapi Bhootaani
Katha Yishyanti Tevya Yaam
Sambhaa Vitasya Chaa Keerti Hi
Maranaa Dati Richyatey

And all people will recount your everlasting dishonour; and to one who has been honoured, dishonour is worse than death.

2:35 Bhayaa Dranaa Dupa Ratam
Mam Syantey Tvaam Mahaa Rathaa Haa
Yey Shaam Cha Tvam Bahu Mataha
Bhootvaa Yaasyasi Laa Ghavam

The mighty chariot warriors will consider that you ran away from the battlefield out of fear, and for those whom you have been held in great esteem you will fall into disgrace.

Additional shlokaas for this leadership lesson in annexure

Leadership Lesson

Inform them of the specific losses of not doing their job, like no growth, no increment, no bonuses, and the possibility of losing their job.

Leadership Shlokaas-10

Duryodhanaa, upon realizing his mistake that he had spent too much time introducing the Paandavaa army, in the following shlokaas switches gear and starts introducing (though briefly) his side to his teacher Dronaachaarya.

1:8 **Bhavaan Bheeshmas Cha Karnas Cha**
Kripas Cha Samitin Jayaha
Ashvat Thaamaa Vikar Nascha
Sauma Dattis Tathai Vacha
Your respected self, Bheeshma, Karna, the ever victorious in battle – Kripa, Ashvat Thaamaa, Vikarna, and the son of Somadatta.

1:9 **Anyecha Bahavash Shooraa Haa**
Madhartey Tyakta Jeevi Taa Haa
Naanaa Shastra Prahara Naa Haa
Sarve Yuddha Vishaara Daahaa

And many other heroes, well skilled in battle, armed with various weapons, missiles and who are determined to give up their lives for my sake.

Leadership Lesson

When you realize that you have made a mistake, acknowledge it and correct it immediately. Remember, you can also learn leadership qualities from Duryodhanaa.

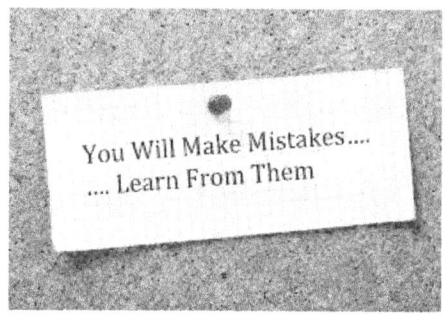

Leadership Shlokaas-11

Sanjayaa, in the following shlokaas, tells Dhritaraashtra what all the soldiers did after Bheeshmaa blew his conch.

1:13 Tatash Shankaas Cha Bher Yascha
Pana Vaanaka Gomukhaa Haa
Sahasai Vaabhya Han Yanta
Sa Shabdas Tumulo Bhavata

Then following Bheeshmaa, conches, kettledrums, tabors, drums, and cow-horns blared forth quite suddenly and the sound in the battlefield was tremendous.

1:14 Tatash Shvetair Hayair Yuktey
Mahati Syan Daney Sthithau
Maadha Vaf Paandavas Chaiva
Divyau Shankhau Pradadh Matuhu

Then, Maadhavaa and the son of Paandu – Arjunaa, seated in their magnificent chariot pulled by white horses blew their divine conches.

1:15 Paancha Janyam Hrishi Kesha Ha
Deva Dattan Dhanan Jaya Ha
Paundrun Dadhmau Mahaa Shan Kham
Bheema Karmaa Vrikodara Ha

Hrishikesha – Krishnaa blew his conch named Paanch Janya, Dhananjaya – Arjunaa blew his conch named Devadatta, Bheemaa the man with a stomach of a wolf, the doer of terrible deeds blew his conch named Paundram.

Additional shlokaas for this leadership lesson in annexure

Leadership Lesson

Team members will mimic or follow what you do as a leader. Be mindful of your actions or words in front of them.

Leadership Shlokaa-12

Krishnaa, in the following shlokaa, tells Arjunaa to do his duty and give up worrying about the results, which will help him remain happy always.

2:51 Kar Majam Buddhi Yuktaa Hi
Phalan Tyak Tvaa Manee Shina Ha
Janma Bandha Vinir Muktaa Haa
Padan Gach Chantya Naa Mayam

Endowed with spiritual intelligence wise men giving up results arising from actions certainly liberate themselves from the bondage of birth and death attaining the state of complete tranquillity & happiness.

Leadership Lesson

Do what you are supposed to do and not worry about the results, as they are not in your control. This will always keep you happy. Focus on the controllable inputs and avoid becoming obsessed with outcomes. Team members love to work for leaders who are always happy and cheerful.

Leadership Shlokaas-13

Krishnaa, in the following shlokaas, tells Arjunaa the secret of bringing out excellence: fighting without having any attachment to the result of the action.

3:7   Yast Vindri Yaani Mana Saa
        Niyam Yaa Rabha Terjuna
        Karmen Driyaik Karma Yogam
        Asaktas Sa Vishish Yatey

But, whosoever, controlling the senses by the mind, O Arjunaa, engages is organs of action in Karma yogaa also called Buddhi yogaa, without attachment, he excels.

3:19   Tas Maad Asaktas Satatam
Kaar Yang Karma Samaa Chara
Asakto Hyaa Charan Karma
Para Maapnoti Poo Rusha Ha

Therefore, always perform actions which should be done, without attachment, for by performing action without attachment, man attains the Supreme.

4:10   Veeta Raaga Bhaya Krodaa Haa
        Man Mayaa Maamu Paa Shritaa Haa
        Bahavo Nyaana Tapa Saa
        Pootaa Mad Bhaava Maa Gataa Haa

Freed from attachment, fear and anger, absorbed in Me, taking refuge in Me, purified by the fire of knowledge, many have attained My being.

Leadership Lesson

To bring out excellence in yourself and your team members, approach the task at hand with 100% commitment, integrity, and joy, without worrying about the outcome. By doing this, you will always be in the present thereby bringing out excellence from within.

Leadership Shlokaa-14

In the following shloka, Krishnaa tells Arjunaa that performing action is essential, as without it, one cannot even meet basic bodily needs, such as food.

3:8   **Niyatang Kuru Karmat Tvam**
        Karma Jyaayo Hya Karmana Ha
        Sha Reera Yaatraa Pichatey
        Na Prasid Dhyey Da Karmana Ha

> *You perform your duty; for action is superior to inaction. Even the maintenance of the body would not be possible for you by inaction.*

Leadership Lesson

Make your team members aware that they must execute their duties, as it directly contributes for the betterment in personal and professional life.

Leadership Shlokaas-15

Krishnaa, in the following shlokaas, tells Arjunaa that his tendencies or past desires are making him act, and he should not take credit for his actions, as he is not the true doer.

3:27 **Pra Kritek Kriya Maa Naani**
Gunaik Karmaani Sar Vasha Ha
Ahan Kaara Vimoo Daatmaa
Kartaa Ham Iti Manyatey

All actions are performed, in all cases, merely by the "Gunaas – Past tendencies". But in ignorance, the soul, deluded by false identification with the body, thinks itself as the doer.

5:8 **Naiva Kinchit Karo Meeti**
Yukto Manyeta Tattva Vita
Pashyan Shrunvan Sprishan Jigran
Ashnan Gach Chan Svapan Shvasan

Those steadfast in Karma yogaa, always think, "I am not the doer," even while engaged in seeing, hearing, touching, smelling, moving, sleeping, breathing.

Leadership Lesson

The organizational goal was achieved because of your team members' efforts, not because of you alone. Therefore, give credit for achievements to them by having regular rewards and recognition functions within the organization.

Leadership Shlokaas-16

Krishnaa, in the following shlokaas, tells Arjunaa that one who does not share the benefits equally with all those who collaborated to achieve the organizational goals is a thief.

3:12 Ishtaan Bhogaan Hivo Devaa Haa
Daash Yantey Yagna Bhaavi Taa Haa
Tairdat Taana Pradaa Yaibhya Ha
Yo Bhunktey Stena Eva Saha

The God's nourished by the sacrifice will give you the desired objects. Indeed, one who enjoys the objects given by the God's without offering in return to them is verily a thief.

3:13 Yagnya Shishtaa Shinas Santa Ha
Muchyantey Sarva Kilbi Shai Hi
Bhunjatey Tey Tvagham Paapaa Haa
Ye Pachan Tyaatma Kaara Naat

The righteous, who share the remnants of the yagnyaa or sacrifice to all equally are freed from all sins, but those sinful ones who cook food for their own sake only, eat only sin.

Leadership Lesson

If you take the credit and the limelight without sharing the glory and benefits with all team members EQUALLY, then you are a thief.

Leadership Shlokaas-17

Krishnaa, in the following shlokaas, tells Arjunaa the consequence of finding faults in his teachings, not having faith, and not implementing the learnings is that one will be destroyed.

3:32   Yetvey Tadabhya Sooyanta Ha
Naanu Tish Tanti Mey Matam
Sarva Nyaana Vimoo Daam Staan
Viddhi Nash Taana Cheta Saha

But those who find faults at My teaching and do not practice it, deluded in all knowledge, and devoid of discrimination, know them to be doomed for destruction

4:40   Agnyas Chaa Shraddha Dhaanas Cha
Samsha Yaat Maa Vinash Yati
Naayan Loko Stina Para Ha
Na Sukham Sam Shayaat Manaha

The ignorant, the faithless, the doubting one goes to destruction. There is no happiness either in this world or the other for the doubter.

Leadership Lesson

Don't keep finding faults and criticizing every decision in the organization without providing possible solutions. If you do, you are on the path to destroying your career & growth within the organization.

Leadership Shlokaa-18

Arjunaa, in the following shlokaas, asks Krishnaa for forgiveness for things he said knowingly or unknowingly, as he was not aware he was talking to Lord Krishnaa, which he realised after seeing the Vishwaroopam–the cosmic form.

11:41 **Sakheti Matvaa Prasabham Yaduktam**
Hey Krishna Hey Yaadava Hey Sakheti
Ajaa Nataa Mahi Maanan Tavedan
Mayaa Pramaa Daat Prana Yena Vaapi
Whatever I have rashly said from carelessness or love, addressing You as O Krishnaa, O Yadavaa, O friend and regarding You merely as a friend, unknowing of this greatness of yours...

11:42 **Yach Chaa Vahaa Saartham Asat Kritosi**
Vihaara Shainyaa Sana Bhoja Neshu
Ekotha Vaapya Chyuta Tat Shamak Sham
Takshaa Mayey Tvaa Maha Mapra Meyam

In whatever way I may have insulted You for the sake of fun, while at play, reposing or sitting, or at meals, when alone (with You), O Achyutaa, or in company – that, O Immeasurable One, I implore you forgive me.

11:43 **Pitaasi Lokasya Charaa Charasya**
Tvamasya Poojyas Cha Gurur Gareeyaan
Natvat Samostya Bhyadhi Kak Kuton Yaha
Lokatra Yepya Pratimap Prabhaava

You are the father of this world, moving and unmoving. You are to be adored by this world. You are the greatest Guru for there exists none who is equal to You; how can there be then another, superior to You in the three worlds, O Being of unequalled power?

Additional shlokaas for this leadership lesson in annexure

Leadership Lesson

Having made a mistake, knowingly or unknowingly, let go of your ego and seek forgiveness. However, don't repeat the same mistake again.

Leadership Shlokaa-19

Krishnaa, in the following shlokaa, is telling Arjunaa not to be afraid of this terrible form but to see it with a cheerful heart.

11:49 Maatey Vyathaa Maacha Vimoodha Bhaava Ha
Drishtvaa Roopam Ghora Meedring Mamedam
Vyapeta Bheef Preeta Manaaf Punas Tvam
Tadeva Mey Roopa Midan Prapashya

Krishnaa tells Arjunaa, be not afraid, nor bewildered on seeing such a terrible form of Mine as this; be free from fear and with a cheerful heart, behold Me once again in My personal form.

Leadership Lesson

Don't run away from reality in all its complexity. Running away will not solve the problem; the more you run from it, the more it will follow you. Face it, solve it, and ensure that the same problem never comes again.

Leadership Shlokaa-20

Krishnaa, in the following shlokaa, tells Arjunaa to have a mentality of sacrifice for the betterment of the society.

16.1 Sri Bhagavaan Uvaa Cha
Abhayam Sat Tvasan Shuddhi Hi
Nyaana Yoga Vyavas Thiti Hi
Daanan Damash Cha Yagnyas Cha
Svaadh Yaayas Tapa Aar Javam

The blessed Lord said:
Fearlessness, purity of heart, established in the wisdom of discrimination of spirit and matter by the science of uniting the individual consciousness with the Ultimate consciousness, charity, control of the senses, **Sacrifice**, *austerity, and alginment...*

16.2 Ahimsaa Satyamak Krodha Ha
Tyaaga Shaanti Rapai Shunam
Dayaa Bhoo Teshva Lolup Tvam
Maar Davam Hree Ra Chaa Palam

...non-violence, truthfulness, absence of anger, renunciation, peacefulness, restraint from fault-finding, compassion towards all living beings, **Freedom from Greed,** *gentleness, modesty, determination - persistency...*

Leadership Lesson

In the interest of the organization, sacrifice personal gains and prioritise the organization first. You may need to sacrifice some facilities or privileges during tough times, but only if you genuinely believe it is a necessity.

Leadership Shlokaa-21

Krishnaa, in the following shlokaa, tells Arjunaa to be truthful to his duty as a Kshatriyaa, which is fighting the war.

16.2   **Ahimsaa Satyamak Krodha Ha**
Tyaaga Shaanti Rapai Shunam
Dayaa Bhoo Teshva Lolup Tvam
Maar Davam Hree Ra Chaa Palam

> ...*non-violence,* **Truthfulness***, absence of anger, renunciation, peacefulness, restraint from fault-finding, compassion towards all living beings, freedom from greed, gentleness, modesty, determination - persistency...*

Leadership Lesson

Be truthful and keep the commitments you make. By keeping up with your commitments, one becomes a trustworthy leader. Team members love to work for leaders who honour their commitments.

Leadership Shlokaa-22

Krishnaa, in the following shlokaa, tells Arjunaa to be free from greed and always think about benefit of others.

16.2   Ahimsaa Satyamak Krodha Ha
        Tyaaga Shaanti Rapai Shunam
        Dayaa Bhoo Teshva Lolup Tvam
        Maar Davam Hree Ra Chaa Palam

> ...*non-violence, truthfulness, absence of anger, renunciation, peacefulness, restraint from fault-finding, compassion towards all living beings, freedom from* **Greed**, *gentleness, modesty, determination - persistency*...

Leadership Lesson

Never be greedy by thinking about yourself and your personal benefits only. Think always about giving benefits to your team members.

Leadership Shlokaa-23

Krishnaa, in the following shlokaa, tells Arjunaa to be modest and not have any pride.

16.2   Ahimsaa Satyamak Krodha Ha
       Tyaaga Shaanti Rapai Shunam
       Dayaa Bhoo Teshva Lolup Tvam
       Maar Davam Hree Ra Chaa Palam

> *...non-violence, truthfulness, absence of anger, renunciation, peacefulness, restraint from fault-finding, compassion towards all living beings, freedom from greed, gentleness,* **Modesty**, *determination - persistency...*

Leadership Lesson

When achieving organizational goals, be humble and downplay yourself. Always stay grounded. Pride comes before a fall.

Leadership Shlokaa-24

Krishnaa, in the following shlokaas, tells Arjunaa not to be a hypocrite, meaning that actions and words should be in sync.

3:6 Karmen Driyaani Sain Yamya
    Ya Aastey Mana Saa Smaran
    Indriyaar Thaan Vimoo Daat Maa
    Mithyaa Chaaras Sa Uchyatey

  He who restraining his sense-organs, sits thinking in his mind of the sense-objects, he, of deluded understanding is called a hypocrite.

16.4 Dambho Darpo Bhi Maanash Cha
    Krodhaf Paa Rushya Meva Cha
    Ag Nyaanan Chaabi Jaa Tasya
    Paartha Sampada Maasu Reem

  Hypocrisy, *arrogance, self-conceit, anger and also harshness and ignorance, arise in one born of the demonic nature, O Arjunaa.*

Leadership Lesson

Ensure that what you say and what you do are aligned and congruent. If you don't you will be called a hypocrite.

Leadership Shlokaa-25

Arjunaa, in the next shlokaas, seeks clarification for his doubt about whether to fight or not. He re-iterates his excuses for not fighting and asks Krishnaa for his help.

2:4 **Arjunaa Uvaa Cha**
Katham Bheeshma Maham Sankhyey
Dronan Cha Madhu Soodana
Ishu Bhir Prati Yots Yaami
Pujaar Haa Vari Soodana
Arjunaa asks Krishnaa:
How, O Madhusoodana shall I, in battle fight with arrows against Bheeshma and Dronaa, who are fit to be worshipped, O destroyer of enemies.

2:5 **Guru Na Hatvaa Hi Mahaanu Bhaavaan**
Shreyo Bhoktum Bhaik Shya Mapiha Lokey
Hat Vaartha Kaamaam Stu Gurooni Haiva
Bhun Jeeya Bhogaan Rudhira Pradig Dhaan
It is better to live in this world by begging, without slaying our great and elevated superiors. By slaying our superiors, the wealth and the pleasurable things which we will enjoy will be tainted in blood.

2:6 **Na Chaitad Vidmak Kataran No Gari Yaha**
Yadvaa Jayema Yadi Vaano Jayey Yuhu
Yaaneva Hatvaa Na Jiji Vishaama Ha
Tevas Thitaaf Pramukey Dhaartha Raashtraa Haa
We do not know what is better for us whether we conquer them, or they conquer us. By slaying the sons of Dhritaraashtra who are standing facing us is it worth us living.

Additional shlokaas for this leadership lesson in annexure

Leadership Lesson

When you are not sure of what to do, whether to act, how to proceed, or when you are confused or have doubts, accept it, let go of your ego, and seek guidance from your seniors or colleagues.

Leadership Shlokaa 26: -

Dhritaraashtra, in the following shlokaa, is alienating his brother's children by using non-inclusive language. He was selfish thinking only about himself and his sons. The result the Kauravaas lost the battle.

1:1 Dhrita Raashtra Uvaa Cha
Dharmak Shetrey Kuruk Shetrey
Sama Vetaa Yuyut Savaha
Maama Kaaf Paanda Vaas Chaiva
Kima Kurvata Sanjaya

Dhritaraashtra is asking Sanjayaa, what are "My sons" and Paandu's son doing after assembling in the Kurukshetra battlefield.

Leadership Lesson

**Use inclusive language & always put organization goals ahead of one's personal, department, & team member's goal.
When you put organizational goals first, you will achieve success and benefit all stakeholders.**

Leadership Shlokaa-27

Arjunaa, in the following shlokaa, is asking Krishnaa for evidence to convince himself that what he is saying is the truth.

4:4 Arjunaa Uvaa Cha
Aparam Bhavato Janma
Param Janma Vivas Vataha
Katham Metad Vijaa Neeyaam
Tva Maadau Prokta Vaaniti

Arjunaa asks:
Later was Your birth, and prior was the birth of Vivasvaan (Sun); how am I to understand that you taught this yoga in the beginning?

Leadership Lesson

Encourage your seniors and team members to provide evidence to further convince yourself that what is committed will indeed be implemented.

Leadership Shlokaas-28

Krishnaa, in the following shlokaas, tells Arjunaa how this knowledge has been transferred from one generation to another, and he is doing the same.

4:1   Sri Bhagavaan Uvaa Cha
Imam Vivas Vatey Yogam
Prokta Vaanaha Mavya Yam
Vivas Vaan Manavey Praaha
Manu Rik Shvaa Kavey Braveet

Lord Krishnaa said:
I taught this imperishable science of uniting the individual consciousness (waves, bubble, froth with the Ultimate Consciousness (ocean unto the Sungod – Surya, Vivasvaan, who taught it unto his son Vaivasvata Manu, who taught it unto his son Ikshvaaku.

4:2   Evam Param Paraa Praaptam
Imam Raajar Shayo Viduhu
Sakaa Leney Ha Maha Taa
Yogo Nashtaf Paran Tapa

In this way the saintly kings came to know this science received by discipline succession; after a great period of time this science of uniting the individual consciousness became lost in this world, O conqueror of the world.

Additional shlokaas for this leadership lesson in annexure

Leadership Lesson

Have a succession plan in place for your personal growth. It is guaranteed that if you develop your team members, you too will grow. If you don't develop your successor, your job is secure, but growth will stop.

Leadership Shlokaas 29: -

Krishnaa, in the following shlokaa, is telling Arjunaa that by doing the job with "Yagnyaa – collaborative spirit," all one's desires will be fulfilled.

3:10   Saha Yag Nyaaf Prajaas Shrist Vaa
        Puro Vaacha Prajaa Patihi
        Anena Prasavish Yadvam
        Eshavos Tvishta Kaama Dhuku

Prajaapati (the Creator) in the beginning of creation created mankind, together with the yagnyaa spirit or sacrifice, thy shall prosper; yagnyaa spirit shall be Kaamadhenu – the all wish fulfilling cow.

3:11　　Devaan Bhaavaya Taa Nena
　　　　Tey Devaa Bhaava Yantuva Ha
　　　　Paras Param Bhaava Yanta Ha
　　　　Shreyaf Parama Vaaps Yathaa

With this yagnyaa spirit may you nourish the Gods, and may those God's nourish you; thus nourishing one another, you shall, attain the Highest God.

Leadership Lesson

Tell all your team members that if they collaborate, play as a team, and achieve organizational goals, all their wishes/desires will be fulfilled, which is guaranteed.

Leadership Shlokaa-30

Krishnaa, in the following shlokaa, tells Arjunaa that one whose mind is fixed on Him all the time is very dear to Him and superior to all.

12:2   Sri Bhagavaan Uvaa Cha
         Maiyaa Veshya Mano Yemaam
         Nitya Yuktaa Upaa Satey
         Shraddha Yaa Parayo Petaa Haa
         Temey Yukta Tamaa Mataa Haa
Lord Krishnaa replied:
Of those who are endowed with firm faith of a special kind beyond material conceptions; fixing the mind on Me, always engaged exclusively worshipping Me, they are considered by me the most superior to all.

Leadership Lesson

One who always thinks about the organization and its growth are considered superior and will always be prioritised for growth within.

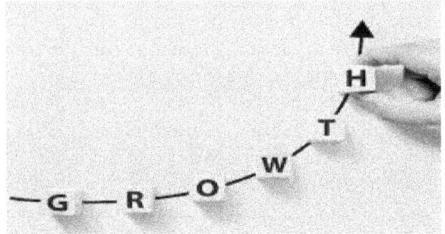

Leadership Shlokaa-31

Krishnaa, in the following shlokaa, tells Arjunaa that even simple offerings like a leaf, flower, fruit or water will make him happy when given with devotion.

9.26   Patram Pushpam Phalam Toyam
       Yomey Bhaktyaa Praya Chati
       Tadaham Bhaktyu Pah Rutam
       Ash Naami Praya Taat Manaha

Whoever offers Me with devotion, a leaf, a flower, some fruit, or water, that I affectionately accept that devotional offering from that pure hearted being.

Leadership Lesson

Look for opportunities to sincerely appreciate your people, which will keep them motivated. It is not always about promotion, increments, or bonuses. Appreciate your team for their personality traits with specific examples, which makes it sincere.

Leadership Shlokaas-32

Krishnaa, in the next shlokaa, tells Arjunaa that life will go on.

4:5 Sri Bhagavaan Uvaa Cha
Bahoo Nimey Vyatee Taani
Jan Maani Tava Chaar Juna
Taan Yaham Veda Sarvaani
Natvam Vet Tha Paran Tapa
Lord Krishnaa replied:
Many births of Mine and of yours have passed O Arjunaa. I am aware of all my births, but you do not know.

4:6 Ajo Pisan Navya Yaat Maa
Bhootaa Naameesh Varo Pisan
Pra Kritin Svaa Madish Taaya
Sambha Vaam Yaatma Maa Yayaa
Though I am unborn and am of imperishable nature, and thought I am the Lord of all beings, yet, ruling over My own nature, I take birth by My own Maayaa.

2:12 Natvey Vaahang Jaatu Naasam
Natvan Nemey Janaadhi Paa Haa
Na Chaiva Na Bhavi Shyaa Maha
Sarvey Vaya Mataf Param

Certainly, never at any time, did I not exist, nor you, nor all these kings and certainly never shall we cease to exist in the future.

Leadership Lesson

Take a break, go on vacation with your family—work will never be over, and the organization will exist whether you are there or not. Going on vacation will humble you and help you stay grounded as you will realize that without you also the organization was functioning.

Leadership Shlokaa-33

Krishnaa, in the following shlokaa, tells Arjunaa all the benefits of fighting the war and the loss of not fighting the war, then tells him to decide, thereby making him accountable for his decision.

18.63   Ititey Nyaana Maakh Yaatam
        Guhyaad Guhya Taram Mayaa
        Vimri Shai Tada Shey Shey Na
        Yathey Chasi Tathaa Kuru

Thus, the wisdom which is a greater secret than all secrets has been declared to you by Me; having reflected upon it fully, you now act as you choose.

Leadership Lesson

Inform your team members of the pros and cons of doing the job or not doing it and ask them to decide whether they want to do it or not. This makes them 100% accountable for their actions.

Section 3
Skill

Every artist was first an amateur.
— Ralph Waldo Emerson

Leadership Shlokaas-34

Arjunaa, in the following shlokaas, tells Krishnaa to return to his original form because he is overwhelmed after seeing the "Vishwaroopam- Cosmic Form."

11:25 Damsh Traa Karaa Laa Nichatey Mukhaani
Dhrist Vaiva Kaalaa Nala Sanni Bhaani
Dishona Jaanena Labhey Cha Sharma
Praseeda Devesha Jagan Nivaasa
Having seen your mouths fearsome with tusks blazing like the Pralaya fires, I know not the four quarters, nor do I find peace: be gracious, O Lord of the Devaas, O Abode of the universe.

11:31 Aakh Yaa Himeko Bhavaan Ugra Roopa Ha
Namos Tutey Deva Vara Praseeda
Vignyaa Tu Mich Chaami Bhavanta Maadyam
Nahi Prajaa Naami Tava Pravrit Tim
Tell me, who You are, so fierce in form? Salutations to You, O God Supreme; have mercy, I desire to know You, the Original Being, I know not indeed Your purpose.

11:45 Adrushta Poorvam Hrishi Tosmi Drishtvaa
Bhayey Nacha Pravya Thitam Mano Mey
Tadeva Mey Darshaya Deva Roopam
Praseeda Devesha Jagan Nivaasa
I am delighted, having seen what I had never seen before, and yet my mind is distressed with fear. Show me your previous form only, O God; have mercy, O God of Gods, O Abode of the Universe.

Additional shlokaas for this leadership lesson in annexure

Leadership Lesson

Once you have shown the BIG picture, some of your employees or team members may get overwhelmed. Make it easy for your team to understand by presenting them the "What" & "How" in simple, clear ways—the small picture.

Leadership Shloka-35

Krishnaa tells Arjunaa the benefit of fighting the war and says that very few people get such a rare opportunity to showcase their skills and achieve their goals in life.

2:32   Yadruch Chayaa Chopa Pannam
Svarga Dvaa Rama Paa Vritam
Sukhi Naha Kshatri Yaaf Paartha
Labhantey Yud Dha Mee Drisham

> *Happy indeed are those Kshatriyaas, O Paartha, who get an opportunity to fight in such a battle, that comes on its own which is an open door to heaven*

Leadership Lesson

Encourage your team members to capitalize on the opportunity to apply their capabilities and skills to prove themselves. Also, explain the specific benefits of doing their job, like growth, increment, bonuses, and the possibility of stock options, etc.

Leadership Shlokaas-36

Krishnaa, in the following shlokaas, tells Arjunaa to have single-minded focus to achieve the desired goal.

4:39 **Shrad Dhaa Vaan Labhatey Nyaanam
Tat Paras Sainya Tendriya Ha
Nyaanam Labdvaa Paraam Shaantim
Achirey Naadhi Gach Chati**
One with full faith, attentively focused, who has conquered the senses, achieves this transcendental knowledge. And having achieved this transcendental knowledge quickly attains supreme peace.

5:17 **Tad Buddha Yas Tadaat Maa Naha
Tan Nish Sthaas Tat Paraaya Naa Haa
Gacch Cantya Punaraa Vrittin
Nyaana Nir Dhoota Kalma Shaa Haa**
Those whose intellect is fixed in God, who are completely absorbed in God, with firm faith in Him as the supreme goal, such persons quickly reach the state from which there is no return, their sins having been dispelled by the light of knowledge.

9.33 **Kim Punar Braah Manaaf Punyaa Haa
Bhaktaa Raajas Shayas Tathaa
Anityama Sukhan Lokam
Imam Praapya Bhajasva Maam**
What then again of devotees, virtuous Braahmins and saintly kings; having taken birth in this transient world full of misery, engage in devotional service unto Me.

Additional shlokaas for this leadership lesson in annexure

Leadership Lesson

Have a single pointed goal and ensure to communicated clearly to each team member. All actions should align towards achieving that single pointed goal. When the river Ganga leaves the Himaalayaa's, it is focused on reaching the Bay of Bengal and never loses sight of its goal.

Leadership Shloka-37

Duryodhanaa, in the next shlokaa, is telling all his soldiers to protect Bheeshma. Duryodhanaa very well knew that Bheeshmaa has got "Itchaa Mrityu," (the power to die at his choice) sending an indirect message to Dronaachaarya that he is dispensable.

1:11   Ayaneshu Cha Sarveshu
           Yathaa Bhaa Gama Vasthi Taa Haa
           Bheeshma Mevaa Bhi Rak Shantu
           Bhavantas Sarva Evahi

All of you stationed in your respective positions should along with taking care of your position should also ensure total protection of Bheeshmaa alone from all strategic points.

Leadership Lesson

Never make your team members feel that they are not important. Ensure every team member feels they are contributing to achieving the organizational goals.

Leadership Shloka-38

Bheeshmaa, after listening to the conversation and realizing that Duryodhanaa is losing his mind and speaking nonsense, blew his conch ("Simha Naadam") to motivate and enthuse him. However, unknowingly, he also declared the war open. The Kauravaas unintentionally declared war.

1:12   Tasya Sanja Nayan Harsham
       Kuru Vrid Dhuf Pitaa Mahaha
       Simha Naadam Vinadyo Chai Hi
       Shankhan Dadhmau Prataa Pavaan

Bheeshmaa the grandsire, the oldest of Kauravaas, to motivate and cheer Duryodhanaa blew his conch like a lion's roar.

Leadership Lesson

Be observant of each team member. When you notice any behaviour change, whether positive or negative, sit with that team member to understand the reason for change. Otherwise, you may be in for a surprise later which could be non-performance or even a resignation.

Leadership Shloka-39

Krishnaa, in the next shlokaa, tells Arjunaa that each one has different approaches to reach the same destination. Some take the knowledge route, some take the action route, and some take the bhakti route.

3:3 Sri Bhagavaan Uvaa Cha
Lokey Smin Dvi Vidaa Nishtaa
Puraa Proktaa Mayaa Nagha
Nyaana Yogena Saankh Yaa Naam
Karma Yogena Yogi Naam

The blessed Lord replied:
In this world there is a twofold path, as I said before, O sinless one, "Saankhya yogaa – the path of knowledge" for intellects and "Buddhi yogaa" for the action-oriented person.

Leadership Lesson

Understand the strengths of each team member and assign tasks accordingly. This way, you won't need to micro-manage—just provide a broad approach. Remember, you recruited them to use their strengths to achieve organizational goals, not to make them perfect.

Leadership Shloka-40

Krishnaa, in the next shlokaa, tells Arjunaa that a person cannot sit idle even for a moment & will be forced to act based on their past desires.

3:5   Nahi Kaschit Shana Mapi
      Jaatu Tish Tatya Karma Kritu
      Kaaryatey Hyava Shak Karma
      Sarvaf Prakriti Jair Gunai Hi

One cannot remain without engaging in activity at any time, even for a moment; certainly, all living beings are helplessly compelled to action by the qualities endowed by the three gunas – saattvic, raajasic, taamasic.

Leadership Lesson

The easiest way to get work done from a non-performing team member is to keep them completely idle—do not call them to any meetings, don't take his opinion, not involve them in anything. As a result, two things can happen: either they will stop complaining and start working, or they will quit. Either way, you will benefit, unless you, as a leader, choose to carry passengers.

Leadership Shlokaa-41

Krishnaa, in the following shlokaa, is telling Arjunaa to take ownership and do what he is supposed to do as a Kshatriyaa, which is to fight the war.

3:35   Shreyaan Sva Dharmo Viguna Ha
       Para Dharmaat Svanush Titaat
       Sva Dharmey Nidhanam Shreya Ha
       Para Dharmo Bhayaa Vahaha

It is far better to perform one's natural prescribed duty, thought tinged with faults, than to perform another's prescribed duty through perfectly. In fact, it is preferable to die in discharge of one's duty than to follow the path of another which is fraught with danger.

Leadership Lesson

Take ownership—think like an owner and do your job, even if it is not perfect. This is better than doing somebody else's job perfectly.

Leadership Shlokaas-42

Krishnaa, in the following shlokaas, tells Arjunaa that he will come at the right time to protect him during tough times.

4:7   Yadaa Yadaa Hi Dharmasya
      Glaanir Bhavati Bhaarata
      Abyu Thaanama Dharmasya
      Tadaat Maanam Sri Jaam Yaham

   Whenever there is decay of righteousness, O Bharataa, and a rise of unrighteousness, then I manifest Myself.

4:8   Parit Traa Naaya Saadhoo Naam
      Vinaa Shaa Yacha Dush Kritaam
      Dharma San Sthaapa Naar Thaaya
      Sambha Vaami Yugey Yugey

   For the protection of good, for the destruction of the wicked and for the establishment of righteousness, I am born at every age.

Leadership Lesson

Tell your team members that you are behind them like a rock during any tough times or when they make mistakes. This pushes your team members to take risks.

Leadership Shlokaa-43

Krishnaa, is the following shlokaa, is telling Arjunaa to go step by step and move towards his goal of attaining the highest.

6:25 **Shanai Shanai Rupara Med
Bud Dhyaa Dhriti Grihee Tayaa
Aatma Samsthan Manak Kritvaa
Na Kinchid Api Chinta Yet**

Little by little, let him attain quietude by his intellect, held firm, having made the mind established in the Self, let him not think of anything.

Leadership Lesson

Have a detailed plan—week by week, fortnightly, monthly, and quarterly —and act on it diligently to achieve the organizational goal.

Leadership Shlokaa-44

Krishnaa, in the following shlokaa, tells Arjunaa to be fearless and fight the war like a Kshatriyaa.

16.1 Sri Bhagavaan Uvaa Cha
      Abhayam Sat Tvasam Shuddhi Hi
      Nyaana Yoga Vyavas Thiti Hi
      Daanan Damash Cha Yagnyas Cha
      Svaadh Yaayas Tapa Aar Javam

The blessed Lord said:
Fearlessness, *purity of heart, established in the wisdom of discrimination of spirit and matter by the science of uniting the individual consciousness with the Ultimate consciousness, charity, control of the senses, sacrifice, austerity, and alginment...*

Leadership Lesson

Be fearless—push your comfort zone and take calculated risks, because you have nothing to lose. You came empty-handed and will leave empty-handed.

Leadership Shlokaa-45

Krishnaa, in the following shlokaa, tells Arjunaa to have a pure heart with no expectations and fight the war.

16.1   Sri Bhagavaan Uvaa Cha
       Abhayam Sat Tvasam Shuddhi Hi
       Nyaana Yoga Vyavas Thiti Hi
       Daanan Damash Cha Yagnyas Cha
       Svaadh Yaayas Tapa Aar Javam

The blessed Lord said:
Fearlessness, **Purity of Heart,** *established in the wisdom of discrimination of spirit and matter by the science of uniting the individual consciousness with the Ultimate consciousness, charity, control of the senses, sacrifice, austerity, and alginment...*

Leadership Lesson

Have a pure mind & heart, and good intentions when dealing with your team members. Don't have any hidden agenda; this will motivate them to go the extra mile for you.

Leadership Shlokaa-46

Krishnaa, in the following shlokaa, tells Arjunaa to restrain from fault finding and to do his duty as a Kshatriyaa.

16.2 Ahimsaa Satyamak Krodha Ha
Tyaaga Shaanti Rapai Shunam
Dayaa Bhoo Teshva Lolup Tvam
Maar Davam Hree Ra Chaa Palam

> ...*non-violence, truthfulness, absence of anger, renunciation, peacefulness,* **Restraint from Fault-finding**, *compassion towards all living beings, freedom from greed, gentleness, modesty, determination - persistency...*

Leadership Lesson

Look for the positives in your team members and in every situation—don't keep finding faults. The bee always finds a flower in a garbage can, while the fly always finds garbage in a flower garden. You will always see what you choose to see.

Leadership Shlokaa-47

Krishnaa, in the following shlokaa, tells Arjunaa to be compassionate toward all living beings.

16.2   Ahimsaa Satyamak Krodha Ha
Tyaaga Shaanti Rapai Shunam
Dayaa Bhoo Teshva Lolup Tvam
Maar Davam Hree Ra Chaa Palam

> ...*non-violence, truthfulness, absence of anger, renunciation, peacefulness, restraint from fault-finding,* **Compassion towards all Living Beings**, *freedom from greed, gentleness, modesty, determination - persistency...*

Leadership Lesson

Be compassionate & caring with all your team members. Help them in times of need, both personally and professionally, thereby strengthening your relationship with them.

Leadership Shlokaa-48

Krishnaa, in the following shlokaa, tells Arjunaa to be patient & determined and to never give up.

16.2   Ahimsaa Satyamak Krodha Ha
Tyaaga Shaanti Rapai Shunam
Dayaa Bhoo Teshva Lolup Tvam
Maar Davam Hree Ra Chaa Palam

> ...*non-violence, truthfulness, absence of anger, renunciation, peacefulness, restraint from fault-finding, compassion towards all living beings, freedom from greed, gentleness, modesty,* **Determination – Persistency.**

Leadership Lesson

Be determined, patient, & persistent in coaching your team members, helping them achieve their professional & personal goals, which in turn will help you achieve yours. If you are not patient, you will become a patient.

Leadership Shlokaa-49

Krishnaa, in the following shlokaa, tells Arjunaa to act with vigour, energy, and enthusiasm.

16.3 Tejak Shamaa Dhritis Shaucham
Adroho Naati Maa Nitaa
Bhavanti Sam Padan Daiveem
Abhi Jaa Tasya Bhaarata

> ... *Vigour, forgiveness, fortitude, cleanliness, freedom from envy, absence of vanity, these arise in one born of the divine nature.*

Leadership Lesson

Any task you take up, ensure you do it with vigour, energy, and enthusiasm. If you find the task boring, take a break. If after the break you still find it boring, then quit. Don't drain the vigour, energy, and enthusiasm of other team members.

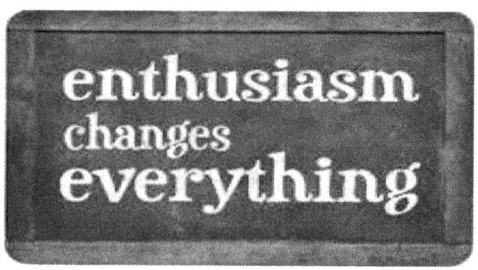

Leadership Shlokaa-50

Krishnaa, in the following shlokaa, tells Arjunaa to keep his mind clean, with no negative and de-motivating thoughts.

16.3   Tejak Shamaa Dhritis Shaucham
        Adroho Naati Maa Nitaa
        Bhavanti Sam Padam Daiveem
        Abhi Jaa Tasya Bhaarata

> ...*vigour, forgiveness, fortitude, **Cleanliness**, freedom from envy, absence of vanity, these arise in one born of the divine nature.*

Leadership Lesson

Keep your mind clean, as well as the environment you work in, including your desktop screen and workstation. This helps clear your thoughts and make the right decisions.

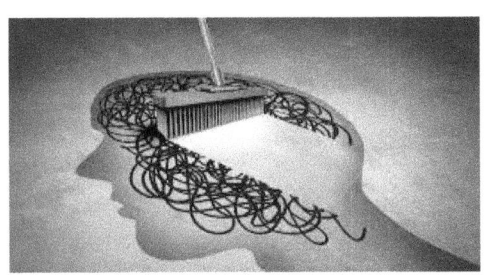

Leadership Shlokaa-51

Krishnaa, in the following shlokaa, tells Arjunaa to be happy when others succeed and not harbour any envy toward them.

16.3 Tejak Shamaa Dhritis Shaucham
Adroho Naati Maa Nitaa
Bhavanti Sam Padam Daiveem
Abhi Jaa Tasya Bhaarata

> *...vigour, forgiveness, fortitude, cleanliness,* **Freedom from Envy**, *absence of vanity, these arise in one born of the divine nature.*

Leadership Lesson

Be happy when your colleagues or subordinates receive promotions or recognition in the organization. Don't feel jealous or harbour bitterness toward them.

Don't envy others, be inspired

Leadership Shlokaa-52

Krishnaa, in the following shlokaa, tells Arjunaa not to have vanity.

16.3   **Tejak Shamaa Dhritis Shaucham**
          Adroho Naati Maa Nitaa
          Bhavanti Sam Padam Daiveem
          Abhi Jaa Tasya Bhaarata

*…vigour, forgiveness, fortitude, cleanliness, freedom from envy, **Absence of Vanity**, these arise in one born of the divine nature.*

Leadership Lesson

Eliminate vanity. Don't keep talking about your achievements in every meeting or every opportunity you get to speak. This will only irritate your team members.

Leadership Shlokaa-53

Arjunaa, in the next shlokaa, is asking Krishnaa for clear direction on what needs to be done by him and which path to take.

5:1 Arjunaa Uvaa Cha
　　Sannyaa Sang Karma Naam Krishna
　　Punar Yogancha Sham Sasi
　　Yacch Reya Yeta Yorey Kam
　　Tanmey Broohi Sunish Chitam

Arjunaa asks:
O Krishnaa, you praised karma sanyaasa – the path of renunciation of action, and You also advised to do Karma yogaa (work with devotion). Please tell me decisively which of the two is more beneficial.

Leadership Lesson

Be crystal clear with your expectations, timelines, and instructions, when assigning tasks to your team members.

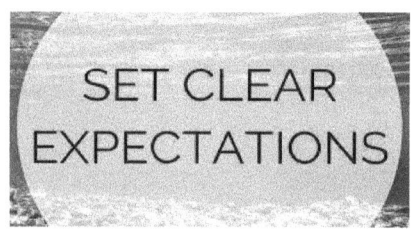

Leadership Shlokaas-54

Krishnaa, in the following shlokaas, tells Arjunaa that whatever one asks or desires from Him, they shall be given.

4:11   Ye Yathaa Maam Prapad Yantey
        Taam Stha Thaiva Bhajaam Yaham
        Mama Vart Maanu Vartantey
        Manush Yaaf Paartha Sarvasha Ha

In whatever way men approach Me, even so do I reward them, all men tread My path in all ways, O son of Pritha.

7:21   Yoyo Yaam Yaan Tanum Bhakta Ha
        Shraddha Yaar Chitu Mich Chati
        Tasya Tasyaa Chalaam Shrad Dhaam
        Taa Meva Vida Dhaam Yaham

Whichever demigod a particular devotee desires with faith & worship, I surely sustain firmly that faith in him.

7:22   Satayaa Shraddha Yaa Yuktaha
        Tasyaa Raa Dhana Mee Hatey
        Labhatey Chatatak Kaa Maan
        Ma Yaiva Vihitaan Hitaan

Endowed with that firm faith the devotee executes worship of the demigods and sanctioned by Me solely, obtains that which he desired from the demigod.

Additional shlokaas for this leadership lesson in annexure

Leadership Lesson

Everything in life is a vibration. The mental vibration that one tunes into is what will materialize. Be mindful of the thoughts running through your mind because they turn into words, based on which you will act, which is what will materialize.

Leadership Shlokaa-55

Vyaasaa, in the following shlokaa, introduces Arjunaa to a new yogaa called "Buddhi Yogaa," which is nothing but "Karma Yogaa" with a different name. The reason he using a new word called "Buddhi Yogaa" is to ensure that Arjunaa pays attention to what is going to be told to him till the end.

2:39   Aey Shaatey Bihitaa Saankhyey
Buddhir Yogey Tvi Maam Shrinu
Bud Dhyaa Yukto Yayaa Paartha
Karma Bandham Prahaa Syasi

O Arjunaa, I have explained to you this spiritual intelligence regarding the nature of the soul – Saankhya yogaa; now listen to this science of action without fruitive desires– Buddhi yogaa, releasing you from the bondage of reactions of actions.

Leadership Lesson 46

Keep a curiosity factor always in your communication so that your team members are actively listening to you till the end, to ensure correct implementation of the plan.

Leadership Shlokaa-56

Krishnaa, in the following shlokaa, tells Arjunaa to do his duty as a Kshatriyaa — to fight — and not worry about the results, which are beyond his control.

2:47 Karmanyey Vaadhi Kaa Rastey
Maa Phaley Shu Kadaa Chana
Maa Karma Phala Hetur Bhoo Hoo
Maatey Sangos Tva Karmani

Your right is to work only, but never to its fruits; let not the fruit-of-action be your motive, nor let the attachment be to inaction.

Leadership Lesson

Ask your team members about the causes, not the effects, as there are too many factors involved to get the effect. If you keep asking for effect from your team members, they might compromise on the ethics and values of the organization & also make wrong commitments to the stakeholders.

Leadership Shlokaa-57

Duryodhanaa knew that Dronaachaarya had trained both the Kauravaas and Paandavaas in the art of warfare, knew each one personally, and understood their capabilities. Duryodhanaa, heart of his heart, knew that what he was fighting for was wrong and unrighteous because of which he was mentally upset and had lost his discriminatory powers due to which he talks nonsense to his teacher. He sarcastically told Dronaacharya that he did not know how to select his students, calling him a Brahmin—indicating that he had only book knowledge, not practical knowledge.

1:3   Pashyai Taam Paandu Putraa Naam
        Aa Chaarya Mahateen Chamoom
        Vyudaan Drupada Putrena
        Tava Shishyena Dhee Mataa

O respected teacher, let me introduce the Paandavaa side to you, please see the mighty army of the Paandavaas arranged in military formation by your intelligent disciple, Dhristadyumnaa – the son of Drupadaa.

1:7   Asmaa Kantu Vishish Taayey
        Taani Bodha Dvij Jot Tama
        Naa Yakaa Mama Sain Yasya
        Sain Yaartan Taan Bravee Mitey

O best of the twice born (Brahmin), please note those who are especially qualified amongst us to lead my military forces, I shall name them for your information.

Leadership Lesson

When you are mentally upset, keep your mouth shut. Give yourself a cooling period of 24 hours before speaking. Don't send emails when you are mentally upset.

Leadership Shlokaa-58

Duryodhanaa, in the following shlokaas, introduces the Paandavaa side soldiers and their capabilities in detail. This goes to show that he has lost his confidence and is preparing the ground for justifying why he lost the war. This conversation is being heard by the Kauravaa soldiers, demotivating them.

1:4   Atra Shooraa Mahesh Vaasaa Haa
       Bhee Maarjuna Samaa Yudhi
       Yuyu Dhaano Viraatas Cha
       Drupadas Cha Mahaa Rataha

   From the Paandavaa side in the battlefield are great bowmen equal to Bheema and Arjunaa, Saatyaki, King Viraata, and the mighty chariot warrior, Drupadaa.

1:5   Dhrista Kethush Cheki Taa Naha
       Kaashi Raajas Cha Veerya Vaan
       Purujit Kunti Bhojas Cha
       Shaibh Yascha Nara Pun Gavaha

   Dhristaketu, Chekitaana, the powerful king of Kaashi, Purujit, Kuntibhoja, and King Shaibhya, the noblest of men.

1:6   Yudhaa Manyus Cha Vikraan Taha
       Uttamau Jaascha Veerya Vaan
       Sau Bhadro Draupadey Yaas Cha
       Sarva Eva Mahaa Rataa Haa

   The valiant Yudhaamanyu, the courageous Uttamaujaa, Abhimanyu the son of Subhadraa, and the sons of Draupadi; certainly, all of them are mighty warriors.

Leadership Lesson

Don't spend too much time talking about your competitors and their strengths. Instead, focus on strengths, and capabilities of your organization, products to motivate your team members.

Leadership Shlokaas-59

In the following shlokaas, Arjunaa is giving his excuses for not fighting the war with his justification to Krishnaa and Krishnaa was just listening to him patiently without interrupting or providing solutions.

1:29 Seedanti Mama Gaa Traani
Mukhan Cha Pari Shush Yati
Vepa Thuscha Sharire Mey
Roma Harshas Cha Jaa Yatey

> *…my limbs are losing its strength, my mouth is drying up, my body is trembling and the hair on my body is standing on its end…*
>
> *Arjunaa after seeing all his relative standing in the opposite side to be killed gives his first bodily excuse for not fighting the war*
> **Excuse number one** *for not performing his duties.*

1:30 Gaan Deevam Shram Satey Hastaat
Tvak Chaiva Pari Dah Yatey
Nacha Shak Nomya Vasthaa Tum
Bhrama Tee Vacha Mey Manaha

> *My bow Gaandeeva is slipping from my hands, my skin is burning, I am unable to stand, and my mind is whirling around.*
>
> *Arjunaa in this shloka continues giving his bodily excuse for not fighting the war.*
> **Excuse number two** *for not performing his duties.*

Additional shlokaas for this leadership lesson in annexure

Leadership Lesson

Be a patient listener when your team members give excuses or talk. Do not interrupt them or provide any solutions immediately.

Leadership Shlokaas-60

In the next shlokaa, Krishnaa, seeing Arjunaa break down, speaks for the first time by asking him a question. He also tells him about the consequence of not fighting the war.

2:2   Sri Bhagavaan Uvaa Cha
      Kutas Tvaa Kash Mala Midam
      Vishamey Samoo Pasthi Tham
      Anaarya Jhus Tamas Svargyam
      Akeerti Kara Marjuna

The blessed Lord asks Arjunaa:
O Arjunaa from where has this illusion of yours appeared in this moment of crisis. This is not befitting honourable men, nor conducive to the attainment of heavenly spheres and is the cause of disgrace.

Leadership Lesson

After listening patiently to your team members, ask questions to bring out the balance excuses, if any. Also tell the team member the loss of not doing their job.

Leadership Shlokaa-61
Ok, change it to what you have written.

In the next shlokaa, Krishnaa, after questioning and telling Arjunaa about the losses of not fighting the war, notices that this has no impact on Arjunaa. To increase the impact of the loss, Krishnaa tells Arjunaa that his behaviour is unmanly.

2:3 Klaibyam Maas Magamaf Paartha
Nai Tatvai Yupa Padyatey
Kshudram Hridaya Daur Balyam
Tyak Tvo Tistha Paran Tapa

O Arjunaa do not yield to unmanliness; this is not worthy of you. O chastiser of enemies giving up this base weakness of heart, get up.

Leadership Lesson

After telling your team member the losses of not doing his or her job, and noticing that they still are not doing it, instil some fear
by mentioning the possibility of the organization downsizing, where they could lose their job. But do this in private only, that too as a final resort.

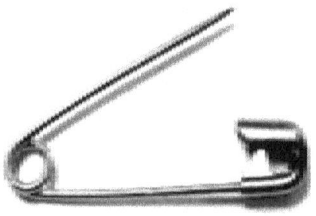

Leadership Shlokaa-62

Krishnaa, in the following shlokaa, after patiently listening to Arjunaa and ensuring all his excuses have been exhausted, and only after Arjunaa asks him explicitly for help (Leadership Lesson 47, shloka 2:7), starts to educate, give advice and solution to Arjunaa.

2:11   Sri Bhagavaan Uvaa Cha
        Asho Chyaan Anva Sochas Tvam
        Prag Nyaa Vaadaams Cha Bhaa Shasey
        Gataa Soona Gataa Sooms Cha
        Naanu Sochanti Panditaa Haa

The blessed Lord replied:
Arjunaa you are grieving for those who need not be grieved for; yet you speak like a 'pandit – a wise man".
A wise man grieves neither for living nor for the dead.

Leadership Lesson

Provide solutions, help, or advice only after being asked explicitly by your team member. Don't volunteer any help because you would be interfering in their past karma.

Leadership Shlokaa-63

Arjunaa, in the following shlokaa, is telling Krishnaa about the negative consequence of fighting the war, acknowledging that it is merely hearsay or gossip.

1:44   Ut Sanna Kula Dharmaa Naam
Manush Yaa Naang Janaar Dana
Narakey Niyatam Vaa Saha
Bhavatee Tyanu Shush Ruma

We have heard, O Janaardhanaa, that it is inevitable that for those men, in whose families the religious practices have been destroyed, dwell in hell for an unknown period.

Leadership Lesson

Don't go by hearsay—speak only with data, else you will lose your credibility and respect within your team members & within the organization.

Leadership Shlokaas-64

Krishnaa, in the following shlokaas, uses a lot of analogies to explain things to Arjunaa to help him make the right decisions as a Kshatriyaa.

2:13 Dehino Smin Yataa Dehey
Kau Maaram Yauva Nang Jaraa
Tataa Dehaan Tara Praap Tihi
Dheeras Tatra Na Muhyati

Just as in this body the embodied (soul) passes into childhood, youth, and old age. So also does the soul passes into another body; the wise man knows it and does not grieve at it.

2:22 Vaa Saamsi Jeer Naani Yathaa Vihaaya
Navaani Grih Naati Naro Paraani
Tathaa Sharee Raani Vihaaya Jeer Naani
Anyaani Sain Yaati Navaani Dey Hee

Just as a man giving up old worn-out garments or garments not useful for an occasion accepts other new apparel, the same way the embodied soul gives up the old or not useful body and takes up a new body.

2:58 Yadaa Sam Haratey Chaayam
Koormo Gaaneeva Sarvasha Ha
Indriyaani Indriyaar Thebhya Ha
Tasya Prag Nyaa Pratish Titaa

When, like the tortoise which withdraws its limbs from all sides, he withdraws his senses from the sense-objects then his wisdom becomes steady.

Additional shlokaas for this leadership lesson in annexure

Leadership Lesson

When communicating with your team members, use analogies to help them understand and make the right decisions. An analogy is method to link an unknown to a known.

Leadership Shlokaas-65

Krishnaa, in the following shlokaas, gives Arjunaa a lot of evidence to convince him to get up and fight the war.

3:20 **Karma Naiva Hisan Siddhim
Aas Thitaa Janakaa Daya Ha
Loka Sangra Hamey Vaapi
Sam Pashyan Kartu Marhasi**

Janakaa and others attained Perfection verily by action only; even with a view of protecting the masses you should perform action.

3:22 **Namey Paar Thaasti Kartav Yam
Trishu Lokeshu Kin Chana
Naana Vaapta Mavaap Tavyam
Varta Evacha Karmani**

There is nothing in the three worlds, O Paartha, that must be done by Me, nor is there anything unattained that should be attained by Me, yet I engage Myself in action.

3:23 **Yadi Hya Hanna Vartey Yam
Jaatu Karmanya Tandrita Ha
Mama Vart Maanu Vartantey
Manush Yaaf Paartha Sar Vashaha**

For, should I not ever engage Myself in action, without relaxation, men would in every way follow My path, O son of Pritha.

Additional shlokaas for this leadership lesson in annexure

Leadership Lesson

Provide a lot of evidence when communicating with your team members. Give examples of employees from within the organization who did a great job and got recognition & growth to convince them to act and do their best.

Leadership Shlokaas-66

Krishnaa, in the following shlokaas, when Arjunaa complains, agrees with him about the difficulty of controlling the mind, then provides a solution on how to control it.

6:33   Arjunaa Uvaa Cha
        Yoyam Yogas Tvayaa Prokta Ha
        Saam Yena Madhu Soodana
        Etasyaa Hanna Pashyaami
        Chanchala Tvaat Stithim Sthiraam

Arjunaa expresses doubt:
This yoga of equanimity is taught by Thee, O slayer of Madhu, I don't see its enduring continuity, because of the restlessness of the mind

6:34   Chanchalam Hi Manak Krishna
        Pra Maathi Balavad Dridam
        Tasyaa Ham Nigra Ham Manyey
        Vaayo Rivasu Dush Karam

The mind verily is, O Krishnaa, restless, turbulent, strong and unyielding, I see it quite difficult to control as the wind.

6:35   Sri Bhagavaan Uvaa Cha
        Asam Shayam Mahaa Baaho
        Mano Durni Grahan Chalam
        Abhyaa Senatu Kaunteya
        Vairaag Yey Nacha Grihya Tey

The blessed Lord answers Arjunaa's query: Undoubtedly, O mighty armed one, the mind is difficult to control and is restless; but, by practice, O son of Kunti, and by dispassion (detachment), it is restrained.

The Leadership Lesson

When a team member presents a problem, first acknowledge their concern, then show them how to overcome the issue, using evidence to support your approach.

Leadership Shlokaas-67

Krishnaa, in the following shlokaas, is telling Arjunaa that he is once again going to tell him what he had told earlier.

10:1   Sri Bhagavaan Uvaa Cha
       Bhooya Eva Mahaa Baaho
       Srunu Mey Paramam Vacha Ha
       Yattey Ham Preeya Maa Naaya
       Vak Shyaami Hita Kaam Yayaa

Lord Krishnaa said:
O Arjunaa, just hear once again My paramount instructions which is for your welfare which you have delight in hearing about Me.

14:1   Sri Bhagavaan Uvaa Cha
       Param Bhooyaf Pravak Shyaami
       Nyaanaa Naam Nyaana Muttamam
       Yaj Nyaatvaa Munayas Sarvey
       Paraam Siddhi Mito Gataa Haa

The blessed Lord said:
I will again declare to you that Supreme knowledge, the best of all knowledge, having known which, all the sages have attained Supreme perfection after this life.

18.64   Sarva Guhya Tamam Bhoo Yaha
       Shrunu Mey Paramam Vacha Ha
       Ishto Simey Drida Miti
       Tato Vak Shaami Tey Hitan

Hear again My supreme word, most secret of all; because you are dearly beloved to Me, therefore, I will tell you what is good for you.

Leadership Lesson

Summarize and document what has been discussed with your team members, then circulate it for provide clarity on what needs to be done and within what timelines.

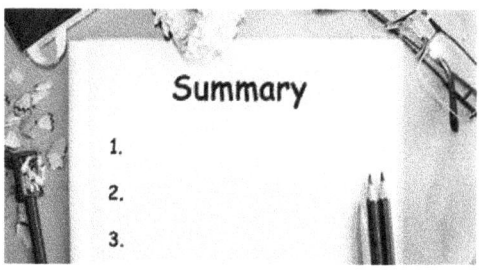

Leadership Shlokaa-68

Krishnaa, in the following shlokaa, tells Arjunaa to be gentle while dealing with people to get the best out of them.

16.2 **Ahimsaa Satyamak Krodha Ha**
Tyaaga Shaanti Rapai Shunam
Dayaa Bhoo Teshva Lolup Tvam
Maar Davam Hree Ra Chaa Palam

> *...non-violence, truthfulness, absence of anger, renunciation, peacefulness, restraint from fault-finding, compassion towards all living beings, freedom from greed,* ***Gentleness****, modesty, determination - persistency...*

Leadership Lesson

Be gentle while communicating with your team members. It is not just what you say, but how you say it that matters. Remember, no one is wrong; each individual has their own viewpoint.

Leadership Shlokaa-69

Krishnaa, in the following shlokaa, tells Arjunaa about the consequence of not following the rules and regulations prescribed in the scriptures; it is wasting his time.

3:16   **Evam Pravar Titang Chakram**
         Naanu Vartaya Tee Haya Ha
         Aghaa Yur Indriyaa Raa Maha
         Mogham Paar Thasa Jeevati

> O Arjunaa, one who in this world does not apply the procedures prescribed and established by the Vedic scriptures, that person living in sin, wastes their human life captivated by sense-gratification.

Leadership Lesson

Ensure that all team members, including yourself, implement policies and follow the processes and procedures. This will ensure effective time management, resulting in organizational growth that benefits all. Otherwise, it is just a waste of time.

Leadership Shlokaa-70

Krishnaa, in the following shlokaa, tells Arjunaa to have no anger.

16.2 Ahimsaa Satyamak Krodha Ha
Tyaaga Shaanti Rapai Shunam
Dayaa Bhoo Teshva Lolup Tvam
Maar Davam Hree Ra Chaa Palam

> ...*non-violence, truthfulness,* **Absence of Anger**, *renunciation, peacefulness, restraint from fault-finding, compassion towards all living beings, freedom from greed, gentleness, modesty, determination - persistency...*

Leadership Lesson

Eliminate anger. The root cause of anger is when expectations exceed reality. The intensity of anger depends on the gap between the two. The larger the gap, more intense the anger. The easiest way to eliminate anger is by telling yourself, "If it happens, ok. If it doesn't happen, that's also ok."

ANGER... Elimination

Leadership Shlokaa-71

Krishnaa, in the following shlokaa, tells Arjunaa that the one who does silent contemplation, meaning one who is de-clutters one's mind, is very dear to him.

12:19 **Tulya Nindaas Tutir Maunee**
Santhus Toyena Kenachit
Aniketas Sthira Mati Hi
Bhakti Maan Mey Priyo Naraha

> ...to whom censure, and praise are equal, who are given to **Silent Contemplation**, content with anything, homeless, steady minded, full of devotion, that man is dear to Me.

Leadership Lesson

Take some quiet time to yourself, declutter your mind, and be at peace with yourself. If you are not happy with yourself, how can you be happy with your team members?

Leadership Shlokaas-72

Krishnaa, in the following shlokaas, tells Arjunaa to look at everybody equally and not discriminate one from another.

5:18 Vidyaa Vinaya Sam Panney
Braah Maney Gavi Hastini
Shuni Chaiva Shvapaa Key Cha
Panditaa Sama Darshi Naha

The truly learned, with the eyes of divine knowledge, see with equal vision a Brahmin, a cow, an elephant, a dog, and a dog-eater.

6:9 Suhrun Mitraa Rudhaa Seena
Madyasta Dhvesh Ya Bandhu Shu
Saadhus Shvapi Cha Paapeshu
Sama Buddhir Vishish Yatey

But more superior is one who with spiritual intelligence acts equally towards natural well-wishers, affectionate well-wishers, enemies, those indifferent to disputes, mediators of disputes, the envious, friends, saintly person as well as a saint.

9.29 Sa Moham Sarva Bhooteshu
Namey Dvesh Yosti Napriya Ha
Ye Bhajanti Tumaam Bhaktyaa
Mayitey Teshu Chaapya Ham

I am equally disposed to all living entities; there is neither friend nor foe to Me; but those who with loving sentiments render devotional service unto Me, such persons are in Me and I am in them.

Leadership Lesson

Treat all your team members equally and avoid favouritism, as it will demotivate others.

Leadership Shlokaas 73: -

Krishnaa, in the following shlokaas, tells Arjunaa the method to be calm, composed and stress free all the time.

2:38 Sukha Dukkhey Samey Kritvaa
Laabhaa Laabhau Jayaa Jayau
Tato Yud Dhaaya Yuj Yasva
Naivam Paapa Mavaap Syasi

Being equipoised in happiness and unhappiness, profit or loss, victory and defeat; thereafter prepare for battle and in this way, you will not incur sinful reaction.

2:48 Yogas Thak Kuru Kar Maani
Sangan Tyak Tvaa Dhanan Jaya
Siddhya Siddhyos Samo Bhootvaa
Samatvam Yoga Uchyatey

Perform actions, O Dhananjayaa, abandoning attachment. Be steadfast and balanced I success and failure. Evenness of mind is called yoga.

2:64 Raaga Dvesha Viyuk Taistu
Vishayaan Indri Yais Charan
Aatma Vashyair Vidhey Yaat Maa
Prasaada Madhi Gach Chati

But the self-controlled man, moving among objects, with his sense under restraint, and free from both attraction and repulsion, attains peace.

Additional shlokaas for this leadership lesson in annexure

Leadership Lesson

Have no expectations from anyone regarding results, and you will remain calm, composed, and stress-free, which will help you think correctly.

Leadership Shlokaa-74

Krishnaa, in the following shlokaa, tells Arjunaa to look for Guru and surrender to him so that he may guide him on the path to wisdom.

4:34   Tad Vid Dhi Prani Paatena
Pari Prash Nena Sevayaa
Upadek Shyanti Tey Nyaa Nam
Nyaa Ninas Tattva Darshina Ha

This knowledge should be learned by accepting a spiritual master and by submissive inquiries and rendering service to him. The self-realized and holy saint endowed with divine revelation will instruct you in wisdom.

Leadership Lesson

Identify a mentor within the organization to show you the path for faster personal and professional growth. Go to the mentor only after exhausting all your methods to address the issue. When you are unable to solve a problem, hold on to people who are capable.

Leadership Shlokaa 75

Krishnaa, in the following shlokaa, is telling Arjunaa to keep on improving his knowledge and along with practice he will reach his goal.

4:38   Nahi Nyaa Nena Sad Risham
         Pavitra Miha Vidyatey
         Tat Svayam Yogasam Siddha Ha
         Kaaley Naat Mani Vindati

> *In this world, there is nothing as purifying as divine knowledge. One who has attained purity of mind through prolonged practice of yoga, receives such knowledge within the heart in due course of time.*

Leadership Lesson

Continuously upgrade your knowledge and skills, and with regular practice, these will become second nature to you. This will not only secure your job but also make you a candidate for growth within the organization.

Leadership Shlokaas-76

Krishnaa, in the following shlokaas, does a root cause analysis for knowing the cause of self-destruction.

2:62 Dhyaa Yato Vishayaan Pum Saha
Sangastey Shoopa Jaa Yatey
Sangaat Sanjaa Yatey Kaama Ha
Kaamaat Krodho Bhijaa Yatey

When a man thinks of objects, attachment for them arises; from attachment desire is born; from desire arises anger.

2:63 Krodhaad Bhavati Sam Mohaha
Sam Mohaat Smriti Vib Bhrama Ha
Smriti Bhram Saad Buddhi Naasha Ha
Buddhi Naa Shaat Pranas Yati

From anger comes delusion; from delusion loss of memory; from loss of memory the destruction of discrimination; from destruction of discrimination, he perishes.

The Leadership Lesson: -

Do a root cause or fish bone analysis with your team member to address challenges or problems.
Continuously ask "Why?" five times (or until all answers are exhausted). Once you exhaust all the answers, you will uncover the root cause of the problem.

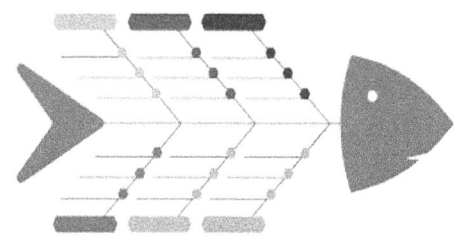

Leadership Shlokaa-77

Krishnaa, in the following shlokaa, is telling Arjunaa that when you rise above the lower desires, material things will not matter.

2:46   Yaavaan Artha Uda Paaney
Sarvatas Samplu Todakey
Taavaan Sarveshu Vedeshu
Braahma Nasya Vijaa Nata Ha

To a Braahmanaa who has known the Self, all the Vedaas are of no use, as is a reservoir of water in a place where there is flood everywhere.

Leadership Lesson

Find your purpose in life. Once you find it, all material things, which are of lower importance, will automatically come to you. To find your purpose, ask yourself this simple question, "If you had all the money in the world, how would you keep yourself occupied?"
Purpose changes behavior.

Annexure
for additional shlokaas of the leadership lessons

Leadership Lesson 1: -

1:23 **Yotsya Maanaa Na Vekshey Ham**
Ya Aey Tetra Samaa Gataa Haa
Dhaarta Raash Trasya Dur Buddhey Hey
Yuddhey Priya Chikeer Shava Ha

For I desire to observe those who are assembled here for the fight, wishing to please in battle the evil-minded sons of Dhritaraashtra.

Leadership Lesson 2: -

11:8 **Natu Maam Shakya Sey Drashtum**
Aney Naiva Svachak Shushaa
Divyan Dadaami Techak Shuhu
Pashya Mey Yoga Maish Varam

But with these present eyes of yours you will not be able to see Me, so I grant you divine sight; behold the omnipotent (all-powerful) majesty of My Ultimate Transcendental Power.

11:9 **Sanjaya Uvaa Cha**
Eva Muk Tvaa Tato Raajan
Mahaa Yogeshvaro Hari Hi
Dar Shayaa Maasa Paar Thaaya
Paramam Roopa Maish Varam

Sanjaya said:
O King, having spoken thus, Lord Krishnaa the sovereign master of all perfecting the science of uniting the individual consciousness with the Ultimate consciousness revealed to Arjunaa the supreme omnipotent (all-powerful) majestic universal form.

11:10 Aneka Vaktra Naya Nam
Anekaad Bhuta Darsha Nam
Aneka Divyaa Bhara Nam
Divyaa Nekod Yataa Yudham

Revealing innumerable wonders, innumerable mouths and eyes, decorated with innumerable dazzling ornaments, armed with innumerable gleaming weapons...

11:11 Divya Maal Yaam Bara Dharam
Divya Gan Dhaanu Lepanam
Sarvaash Charya Mayan Devam
Anantam Vishvato Mukham

...magnificently attired and resplendently garlanded, anointed with exquisite, celestial fragrances, completely amazing and phenomenal, unlimited, brilliant and all pervading.

11:12 Divi Soor Yasa Has Rasya
Bhaved Yuga Padut Thitaa
Yadibhaa Sadrushee Saas Yaad
Bhaasas Tasya Mahaat Manaha

If the effulgence of a thousand suns simultaneously were to blaze forth in the firmament; then that might be comparable with the Ultimate personalities universal form.

Leadership Lesson 9: -

2:36 Avaachya Vaadaams Cha Bahoon
Vadhish Yanti Tavaa Hitaa Haa
Nin Dantas Tava Saamarth Yam
Tato Dukkha Taran Nukim

Your enemies will speak many malicious and insulting words discrediting your prowess. Alas what could be more painful than that?

Leadership Lesson 11: -

1:16 Ananta Vijayam Raajaa
Kuntee Putro Yudhis Thira Ha
Nakulas Saha Devas Cha
Sughosha Mani Pushpa Kau

King Yudhishthira, the son of Kunti, blew the Ananta Vijaya, Nakula and Sahadeva blew Sughosha and Mani Pushpakau, respectively.

1:17 Kaashyas Cha Paramesh Vaa Saha
Shikhandi Cha Mahaa Rataha
Dhrista Dyumno Viraatas Cha
Saatya Kishchaa Paraa Jitaha

The king of Kaashi – an excellent archer, Shikhandi – the mighty commander, Dhritadyumna, Viraata, and Saatyaki – the unconquered.

1:18 Drupado Draupadey Yaas Cha
Sarva Shaf Prithi Vee Patey
Sau Bhadras Cha Mahaa Baa Huhu
Shankhaan Dadhmuf Prithak Pritha Ka

Drupada and the sons of Draupadi, and the son of Subhadraa blew their respective conches one after another.

3:21 Yad Yadaa Charati Shresh Taha
Tatta Devey Taro Jana Ha
Sayat Pramaa Nang Kurutey
Lokas Tadanu Vartatey

Whatever a great man does, that other men also imitate; whatever he sets up as the standard, that the people in the world will follow.

3:26 Na Buddhi Bhedan Janayedh
Ag Nyaa Naang Karma Sangi Naam
Josha Yet Sarva Karmaani
Vidvaan Yuktas Samaa Charan

Let no wise man unsettle the minds of ignorant people, who are attached to action for results; he should engage them in all actions, himself fulfilling them without attachment. Sanjayaa & Krishnaa are telling that whatever the elder's or leaders do, that is what his soldiers or followers will do or follow.

Leadership Lesson 18: -

11:44 Tasmaat Pranamya Prani Dhaaya Kaayam
Prasaa Dayey Tvaa Maha Meesha Meedyam
Piteva Putrasya Sakheva Sakh Yuhu
Priyaf Priyaa Yaar Hasi Deva Sodum

Therefore, bowing down, prostrating my body, I crave your forgiveness, adorable Lord. As a father forgives his son, a friend his friend, a lover his beloved, even so should You forgive me, O Deva.

16.3 Tejak Shamaa Dhritis Shaucham
Adroho Naati Maa Nitaa
Bhavanti Sam Padan Daiveem
Abhi Jaa Tasya Bhaarata

*…vigour, **Forgiveness**, fortitude, cleanliness, freedom from envy, absence of vanity, these arise in one born of the divine nature.*

Leadership Lesson 25: -

2.7 Kaar Panya Dosho Pahatas Svabhaa Vaha
Prichaami Tvaam Dharma Samooda Chetaa Haa
Yashrey Yas Yaan Nischi Tam Broohi Tanmey
Shis Yastey Ham Shaadhi Maam Tvaam
Prapan Nam

My heart is overpowered by the taint of pity, my mind is confused as to doing my duty. I ask thee, please tell me decisively what is good for me. I am your disciple, please instruct me as I have taken refuge in you.

2:8 Nahi Prapash Yaami Mamaa Panud Yaad
Yaccho Ka Muccho Shanam Indriyaa Naam
Avaapya Bhoomaa Vasa Patna Mrid Dham
Raajyam Suraanaa Mapi Chaadhi Patyam

Even after obtaining a prosperous and unrivalled kingdom on the earth. And supremacy of even the demigods; I do not see that which can dispel this grief of mine which is draining my senses.

3:1 Arjunaa Uvaa Cha
Jyaa Yasee Chet Karma Nastey
Mataa Buddhir Janaar Dana
Tat King Karmani Ghorey Maam
Niyo Jayasi Keshava

Arjunaa asks:
Taught by you that knowledge is superior to action, O Janaardhana, why then do you, O Keshavaa tell me to take this terrible action?

3:2 Vyaamish Reneva Vaak Yena
Buddhim Mohaya Seeva Mey
Tadekam Vadanish Chitya
Yena Shreyo Hamaap Nuyaam

My spiritual intelligence is certainly becoming confused by your words of conflicting conclusions; therefore, ascertaining one of them, please reveal that by which I may obtain the greatest benefit.

18:1 Arjunaa Uvaa Cha
Sannyaa Sasya Mahaa Baaho
Tattva Mich Chaami Veditum
Tyaagas Yacha Hrishi Kesha
Prithak Keshini Shoodana

Arjunaa asks: O mighty armed one, O master of the senses, O slayer of Keshi demon, I wish to understand the factual distinction between renunciation (Sanyaasa) and the renunciation of the fruits of action (Tyaaga).

Leadership Shlokaas 28: -

4:3 Sa Aey Vaayam Mayaa Tedya
Yogaf Proktaf Puraa Tanaha
Bhakto Simey Sakhaa Cheti
Raha Syan Yetad Uttamam

This very same ancient science of uniting the individual consciousness with the Ultimate consciousness and which is a supreme secret; therefore, is being described by Me unto you today because you are My devotee and friend.

18.68 Ya Imam Paramang Guhyam
Mad Bhaktes Vabhi Daas Yati
Bhaktim Mayi Paraang Kritvaa
Maamey Vais Yatya Sam Shaya Ha

He who, with supreme devotion to Me, will teach this supreme secret to My devotees, shall doubtless come to Me.

Leadership Lesson 34: -

11:46 Kireetinan Gadinan Chakra Hastam
Icchaa Mitvaan Drashtu Mahan Tathaiva
Tenaiva Roopena Chatur Bhujena
Sahasra Baaho Bhava Vishva Moortey

I desire to see You as before, crowned, bearing a mace, with a discuss in hand, in Your former form only, having four arms, O thousand-armed, O universal form.

Leadership Lesson 36: -

9.34 Man Manaa Bhava Mad Bhakta Ha
Madyaaji Maan Namas Kuru
Maamey Vaishyasi Yuktvai Vam
Aat Maanam Mat Paraa Yanaha

Me, sacrifice to Me, bow down to Me, having thus united your whole self with Me, taking me as the Supreme goal, you shall come to Me.

12:3 Yey Tvakshara Manir Deshyam
Avyak Tam Paryu Paa Satey
Sarvatra Gama Chintyan Cha
Koo Tastam Achalan Dhruvam

Those who worship the imperishable, the indefinable, the unmanifest, the omnipresent, the unthinkable, the unchangeable, the immovable and the external...

12:4 San Niyam Mendriya Graamam
Sarvatra Sama Buddha Yaha
Tey Praap Nuvanti Maa Meva
Sarva Bhoota Hitey Rataa Haa

...having restrained all the senses, even-minded everywhere, rejoicing ever, in the welfare of all beings, verily, they also come to Me.

18.65 Man Manaa Bhava Mad Bhakta Ha
Madyaaji Maan Namas Kuru
Maamey Vaish Yasi Satyan Tey
Prati Jaaney Priyo Simey

Fix your mind upon Me; be devoted to Me; sacrifice for Me; bow down to Me; you shall come, surely then, to Me alone; truly do I promise to you for you are dear to Me.

Leadership Lesson 54: -

8.5 Anta Kaaley Cha Maa Meva
Smaran Muktvaa Kaley Varam
Yaf Prayaati Samad Bhaavam
Yaati Naast Yatra Samshaya Ha

And whosoever, leaving the body, goes forth remembering Me alone, at the time of death, he attains My being; there is no doubt about this.

8.6 Yam Yam Vaapi Smaran Bhaavam
Tyajat Yantey Kaley Varam
Tanta Mey Vaiti Kaunteya
Sadaa Tad Bhaava Bhaa Vitaha

Whosoever, at the end, leaves the body, thinking of any being, to that being alone he goes, O Kaunteya (son of Kunti), because of his constant thought of that being.

9.25 Yaanti Deva Vrataa Devaan
Pitruu Nyaanti Pitra Vrataa Haa
Bhootaani Yaanti Bhootej Yaa Haa
Yaanti Madyaaji Nopi Maam

Worshipers of the demigods, worshipers of the ancestors go to the ancestors, worshipers of the ghosts and spirits go to the ghosts and spirits & My worshipers certainly come to Me.

Leadership Lesson 59: -

1:31 Nimi Taani Cha Pash Yaami
Viparee Taani Keshava
Nacha Shreyo Nupash Yaami
Hatvaa Svajana Maa Havey

And I see bad omens, O Keshavaa. Nor do I see any good in killing my own people in the battle.
Arjunaa in this shloka starts to give his first mental excuse for not fighting the war.
Excuse number three *for not performing his duties.*

1:32   Na Kaankshey Vijayan Krishna
Nacha Raajyam Sukhaani Cha
Kinno Raaj Yena Govinda
Kin Bhogair Jeevi Tena Vaa

Krishnaa, I do not desire victory, nor kingdom, nor pleasures. Of what use is this kingdom to us, O Govinda? Of what avail are these pleasure and life itself?
Arjunaa in this shloka continues giving his mental excuse for not fighting the war.
Excuse number four *for not performing his duties.*

1:33   Yeshaa Marthey Kaank Shitan Naha
Raajyam Bhogaas Sukhaani Cha
Ta Imay Vasthi Taa Yuddhey
Praanaam Styak Tvaa Dhanaani Cha

For whose sake we desire kingdom, enjoyment, and pleasures are standing here in battle wanting to renounce their life and wealth…

1:34   Aachaar Yaaf Pitaraf Putraa Haa
Stathai Vacha Pitaama Haa Haa
Maa Tulaas Sva Shuraaf Pautraa Haa
Shyaa Laas Sam Bandhi Nas Tataa

…teachers, fathers, sons, grandfathers, maternal uncles, fathers-in-law, grandsons, brothers-in-law and other relatives.

Arjunaa in these two shlokaas continues giving his mental excuse for not fighting the war.
Excuse number five *for not performing his duties.*

1:35　　Etaan Na Hantu Mich Chaami
　　　　Ghna Topi Madhu Soodana
　　　　Api Trailokya Raaj Yasya
　　　　Hey Toh Kimnu Mahee Kritey

I do not wish to kill them even if they wish to kill me. O Madhusoodana, even for the sake of kingdom over the three worlds, leave alone for the sake of earth.

Arjunaa in this shloka continues giving his mental excuse for not fighting the war.
Excuse number six *for not performing his duties.*

1:36　　Nihatya Dhaarta Raash Traan Naha
　　　　Kaa Preetis Syaaj Janaar Dana
　　　　Paapa Mevaa Shrayey Dasmaan
　　　　Hatvai Taanaa Tataa Yinaha

Killing the sons of Dhritaraasthra what pleasure can be ours, O Janaardhana? Sin alone will be our gain by killing them.

Arjunaa in this shloka continues giving his mental excuse for not fighting the war.
Excuse number seven *for not performing his duties.*

1:37　　Tasmaan Naarhaa Vayam Hantun
　　　　Dhaarta Raash Traan Sva Baandha Vaan
　　　　Sva Janam Hi Katham Hatvaa
　　　　Sukinash Syaama Maadhava

Therefore, we shall not kill the sons of Dhritaraashtra, our relatives, for how can we be happy by killing our own people, O Keshavaa?

Arjunaa in this shloka continues giving his mental excuse for not fighting the war.
Excuse number eight *for not performing his duties.*

1:38   Yadya Pyetey Na Pashyanti
       Lobho Pahata Cheta Saha
       Kulak Shaya Kritan Dosham
       Mitra Drohey Cha Paa Takam

   Though they with their intelligence clouded by greed, see no evil in destruction of the families in the society, and see no sin in their cruelty to friends...

1:39   Kathan Na Neya Masmaa Bihi
       Paa Paa Dasmaan Nivarti Tum
       Kulak Shaya Kritan Dosham
       Prapash Yad Bhir Janaar Dana

   ...why should not we, who clearly see evil in the destruction of the family-units, learn to turn away from this sin, O Janaardhana?
   Arjunaa in these two shlokaas continues giving his mental excuse for not fighting the war.
   Excuse number nine *for not performing his duties.*

1:40   Kulak Shayey Pranash Yanti
       Kula Dharmaa Sanaata Naahaa
       Dharmey Nashtey Kulang Krits Nam
       Adharmo Bhi Bhavat Yuta

   With the destruction of the family, the spiritual traditions of the family perish forever, when spiritual values are destroyed then unrighteousness predominates the entire society.

   Arjunaa in this shlokaa continues giving his mental excuse for not fighting the war.
   Excuse number ten *for not performing his duties.*

1:41   Adhar Maabhi Bhavaat Krishna
Pradush Yanti Kulastriya Ha
Stree Shu Dhus Taasu Vaarsh Neya
Jaa Yatey Varna Sankara Ha

O Krishnaa, when unrighteousness is predominant, then women in the family become degraded and from the degradation of womanhood, undesirable progeny comes into existence.

Arjunaa in this shlokaa continues giving his mental excuse for not fighting the war.
Excuse number eleven *for not performing his duties.*

1:42   Sankaro Nara Kaa Yaiva
Kulag Naa Naang Kulasya Cha
Patanti Pitaro Hey Shaam
Lupta Pindo Dakak Kriyaa Haa

Confusion of castes leads the slayer of the family to hell, for their forefathers fall, deprived of the offerings of Pinda (rice balls) and water (libations).

Arjunaa in this shloka continues giving his mental excuse for not fighting the war.
Excuse number twelve *for not performing his duties.*

1:43   Doshai Reytai Kulag Naa Naam
Varna Sankara Kaara Kaihi
Utsaa Dyantey Jaati Dharmaa Haa
Kula Dharmaas Cha Shaash Vataa Haa

By these evil deeds of the destroyers of the family, which cause confusion of castes, the eternal religious rites of the caste and the family are destroyed.

Arjunaa in this shloka continues giving his mental excuse for not fighting the war.
Excuse number thirteen *for not performing his duties.*

1:46 Yadi Maama Pratee Kaaram
Ashas Tram Shastra Paanaya Ha
Dhaarta Raashtraa Raney Han Yuhu
Tanmek Shema Taram Bhavet

If the sons of Dhritaraashtra with weapons in hand, kill me in battle, unresisting, unarmed that would be better for me.

Arjunaa in this shloka continues giving his mental excuse for not fighting the war.
Excuse number fourteen *for not performing his duties.*

1:47 Sanjaya Uvaa Cha
Eva Muk Tvaar Junas Sankhey
Ratho Pasta Upaa Vishata
Vis Rijya Sasharan Chaapam
Sho Kasam Vigna Maana Saha

Sanjayaa tells Dhritaraashtra:
Having thus spoken in the middle of the battlefield, Arjunaa sat down on the seat of the chariot, casting away his bow and arrow, with a mind distressed with sorrow.

Leadership Lesson 64: -

2:67 Indriyaa Naamhi Chara Taam
Yan Mano Nuvi Dheeyatey
Tadasya Harati Prag Nyaam
Vaayur Naavami Vaam Bhasi

For, the mind, which follows in the wake of the wandering senses, carries away his discrimination, as the wind carries away a boat on the waters.

3:38 Dhoomey Naa Vriyatey Van Nihi
Yathaa Darsho Maley Nacha
Yathol Benaa Vrito Garbha Ha
Tathaa Teney Damaa Vritam

Just a fire is covered by smoke, as mirror by dust and the embryo is covered by the womb; so, this knowledge is covered by desire.

4:37 Yathai Dhaamsi Samid Dhog Nihi
Bhasma Saat Kuru Terjuna
Nyaa Naag Nis Sarva Karmaani
Bhasma Saat Kuru Tey Tathaa

Just as the blazing fire turns wood to ashes; similarly, the fire of this knowledge turns all the reactions from fruitive activities to ashes.

5:10 Brahman Yaa Dhaaya Karmaani
Sangan Tyak Tvaa Karotiya Ha
Lipyatey Nasa Paapena
Padma Patrami Vaam Bhasaa

Those who dedicate their actions to God, abandoning all attachment, remain untouched by sin, just as a lotus leaf is untouched by water

6:19   Yathaa Deepo Nivaa Tastha Ha
       Nain Gatey Sopa Maa Smrutaa
       Yogino Yata Chit Tasya
       Yunjato Yoga Maat Mana Ha

As a lamp placed in a windless place does not flicker is a description of a yogi of controlled-mind practicing yoga (actions without focus on fruits) of the self.

9.6   Yathaa Kaashash Thito Nityam
       Vaayus Sarvatra Go Mahaan
       Tathaa Sarvaani Bhootaani
       Mats Thaanee Tyupa Dhaaraya

Understand just as the mighty wind blowing everywhere is always situated within space; similarly, all created beings thus are situated in Me.

13.32 Yathaa Sarva Gatam Sauksh Myaad
       Aa Kaashan Nopa Lipyatey
       Sar Vatraa Vas Thito Dehey
       Tathaat Maa Nopa Lipyatey

As the all-pervading ether is not tainted, because of its subtlety, so too the Self, seated everywhere in the body, is not affected.

13.33 Yathaa Prakaa Shayat Yekaha
       Kritsnam Loka Mimam Ravihi
       Kshetran Kshetree Tathaa Kritsnam
       Prakaa Shayati Bhaarata

Just as the Sun illumines the whole world, so also the Lord of the field (Paramaatma) illumines the whole field, O Bharataa.

15:8 Shariram Yada Vaap Noti
Yach Chaa Pyut Kraa Matees Varaha
Griheet Vaitaani Sain Yaati
Vaayur Gandhaa Nivaa Shayaat

As the air carries fragrance from place to place, so does the embodied soul carry the mind and senses with it, when it leaves an old body and enters a new one.

Leadership Lesson 65: -

7:8 Raso Hamapsu Kaunteya
Pra Bhaasmi Shashi Soorya Yoho
Pranavas Sarva Vedeshu
Shabdak Key Pau Rushan Nrishu

O Arjunaa, I am the sweetness in water, the radiant luster of the sun and the moon, I am the syllable Om in all the Vedas, sound in ether, and ability in men.

7:9 Punyo Gandhaf Prithiv Yaancha
Tejas Chaasmi Vibhaa Vasau
Jeevanam Sarva Bhooteshu
Tapash Chaasmi Tapas Vishu

I am the sweet fragrance in earth, and the brilliance in fire, the vitality in all beings, and I am tolerant in those who perform austerity.

7:10 Beejam Maam Sarva Bhootaa Naam
Vid Dhi Paartha Sanaa Tanam
Buddhir Buddhi Mataa Masmi
Tejas Tejas Vinaa Maham

Know me Partha as the eternal seed of all beings; I am the wisdom of the intelligent; the splendor of the splendid things and beings.

7:11 Balam Bala Vataan Chaaham
Kaama Raaga Vivar Jitam
Dharmaa Viruddho Bhooteshu
Kaa Mosmi Bharatar Shabha

Of the strong, I am the strength of the strong devoid of attachment, I am passion and energy of procreation in all living beings which is not contrary to righteousness.

10:21 Aadityaa Naam Aham Vishnu Hu
Jyoti Shaam Raviram Shumaan
Maree Chir Marutaa Masmi
Nakshatraa Naam Aham Shashee

Among the 12 Aadityas, I am Vishnu; among the luminaries, the radiant Sun; I am Marichi among the Maruts; among constellations, I am the moon.

10:22 Vedaa Naam Saama Vedosmi
Devaa Naam Asmi Vaasava Ha
Indriyaa Naam Manash Chaasmi
Bhootaa Naam Asmi Chetanaa

Among Vedaas, I am Saama Vedaa; I am Vaasava, among the gods; among the senses, I am the mind; and I am the intelligence among living beings.

10:23 Rudraa Naam Shan Karash Chaasmi
Vittey Sho Yaksha Raksha Saam
Vasoo Naam Paa Vakash Chaasmi
Merus Shikhari Naa Maham

And among the Rudraas, I am Shankaraa; among the Yakshaas and Raakshas, I am the Lord of wealth – Kuberaa; among the vasus I am Agni, the fire god, and among mountains, I am Meru.

10:24 Purodha Saancha Mukhyan Maam
Vid Dhi Paartha Brahas Patim
Sey Naanee Naam Aham Skanda Ha
Sarasaa Masmi Saagara Ha

Among the household I am priest, know me as Brihaspati; among generals, I am Karthikeyaa; and of reservoirs of water, I am the ocean.

10:25 Maharshee Naam Bhrigu Raham
Giraa Mas Maika Mak Sharam
Yag Nyaa Naan Japa Yaj Nyosmi
Sthaa Varaa Naam Himaalaya Ha

Of the great sages, I am Bhrigu; of speech I am the mono syllable, Om; of all the types of sacrifice, I am the chanting of the holy name of the Ultimate personality and of immovable things, I am the Himaalayan Mountain.

10:26 Ashvat Thas Sarva Vrikshaa Naam
Devarshee Naancha Naarada Ha
Gandhar Vaanaan Chitra Rataha
Siddhaa Naang Kapilo Munihi

Of all the trees, I am the sacred Banyan tree; of divine sages, I am Naarad muni; of the Gandharvaas, I am Chitraratha; and of perfected beings, I am Kapila deva.

10:27 Ucchais Shravasa Mash Vaanaam
Viddhi Maan Amritod Bhavam
Airaa Vatang Gajendraa Naam
Naraa Naancha Naraa Dhipam

Of horses know Me as Ucchaishrava generated from nectar churned in the milky ocean; of lordly elephants, Airaavata; among humans, the king.

10:28   Aayu Dhaa Naam Aham Vajram
        Dhenoo Naam Asmi Kaama Dhuka
        Prajanash Chaasmi Kandar Paha
        Sarpaa Naa Masmi Vaasuki Hi

Of all the weapons, I am thunderbolt; of cows, I am the wish fulfilling cow – Surabhi; of motivation for procreation for begetting progeny, I am cupid; and of poisonous singled headed snakes, I am Vaasuki.

10:29   Anantash Chaasmi Naagaa Naam
        Varuno Yaada Saa Maham
        Pitruu Naa Marya Maa Chaasmi
        Yama Sain Yama Taa Maham

Of the many headed non-poisonous serpents, I am the serpent Ananta; of all the acquatics, I am Varuna the demi-god ruling the inhabitants of water; among ancestors, I am Aaryama; and of administration of justice, I am Yama Raaja, the judge of all beings at the time of death.

10:30   Prahlaa Dash Chaasmi Daityaa Naam
        Kaalak Kalaya Taa Maham
        Mrigaa Naancha Mrigendro Ham
        Vaina Tey Yashcha Pakshi Naam

Of the Daitya, I am Prahalaada; of measurement, I am time; of all animals, I am lion; and of birds, I am Garudaa.

10:31   Pavanaf Pavataa Masmi
        Raamas Shastra Bhrataa Maham
        Jha Shaa Naam Makarash Chaasmi
        Sro Tasaa Masmi Jaah Navi

Of swift moving, I am the wind; of all the wielders of weapons, I am Raama; of all the fishes, I am shark; and of all flowing rivers, I am Gangaa.

10:32　Sargaa Naam Aadi Rantash Cha
　　　　Madhyan Chaivaa Hamar Juna
　　　　Adyaatma Vidyaa Vidyaa Naam
　　　　Vaadaf Pravada Taa Maham

Among creations, I am the beginning, the middle, and also the end; among sciences, I am the science of the Self; and in arguments, I am logic.

10:33　Aksharaa Naam Akaa Rosmi
　　　　Dvandvas Saamaa Si Kasya Cha
　　　　Aha Mevaak Shayak Kaa Laha
　　　　Dhaataa Ham Vishva Tomukha Ha

Among letters, I am the first letter A; among all the compounds, I am the dual (coordinates – bring together); I am truly, the inexhaustible or the everlasting time; I am the all-faced dispenser of the fruits of all actions having faces in all directions.

10:34　Mrityus Sarva Harash Chaaham
　　　　Ud Bhavash Cha Bhavishya Taam
　　　　Keertis Shreer Vaakcha Naari Naam
　　　　Smrittir Medhaa Dhritik Shamaa

And I am all devouring Death; and prosperity of those who are prosperous; among the feminine qualities, I am fame, prosperity, speech, memory, intelligence, firmness and forgiveness.

10:35　Brihat Saama Tathaa Saam Naam
　　　　Gaa Yatree Chanda Saa Maham
　　　　Maasaa Naam Maarga Sheer Shoham
　　　　Ritoo Naang Kusumaa Karaha

Of the Saama vedaa hymns, I am the Brihat Saama; and of mantras composed in poetic meter, I am Gaayatri; of the months, I am harvest; and among seasons, I am spring.

10:36 Dyootan Chalaya Taa Masmi
Tejas Tejas Vinaa Maham
Jayosmi Vyava Saa Yosmi
Sat Tvam Sattva Vataa Maham

Of deceiver, I am gambling; I am the glory of the glorious, I am victory of the victorious; and the nobility of the noble.

10:37 Vrish Nee Naam Vaasu Devosmi
Paandavaa Naam Dhanan Jaya Ha
Munee Naa Mapya Ham Vyaa Saha
Kavee Naam Uusha Naa Kavi Hi

Of the descendants of the Vrishni, I am Vaasudeva; of the Paandavaas, I am Arjunaa; of the sages, I am Vyaasaa deva; among great scholars, I am Sukraacharya, the priest of the Daityas.

10:38 Dando Damaya Taa Masmi
Neeti Rasmi Jigee Shataam
Maunan Chai Vaasmi Guhyaa Naam
Nyaa Nang Nyaana Vataa Maham

Among punishers, I am the rod; among those who seek victory, I am statesmanship; and among all secrets, I am silence; and I am knowledge among knowers.

10:39 Yach Chaapi Sarva Bhootaa Naam
Beejan Tada Hamar Juna
Na Tadasti Vinaa Yat Syaat
Mayaa Bhootan Charaa Charam

And I am the seed of all beings, that also I am, O Arjunaa; there is no being, whether moving or nonmoving that can exist without Me.

10:41 Yadyad Vibhooti Mat Sat Tvam
Shrimad Oorjita Meva Vaa
Tatta Devaa Vagach Chatvam
Mama Tey Jonsha Sam Bhavam

Whatever it is that is glorious, prosperous, or powerful in any being, know that to be a manifestation of a part of My splendor.

Leadership Lesson 73: -

2:71 Vihaaya Kaamaan Yas Sarvaan
Pumaam Charati Nih Spriha Ha
Nir Mamo Nirahan Kaa Raha
Sa Shaanthi Madhi Gach Chati

That man attains peace who, abandoning all desires, moves about without longing, without the sense of "I-ness" and "my-ness".

4:21 Niraa Sheer Yata Chit Taat Maa
Tyakta Sarva Pari Graha Ha
Shaaree Rang Kevalang Karma
Kurvan Naap Noti Kilbhi Sham

Without expectations, with a self-controlled mind, having abandoned all possessions, doing merely bodily actions, he incurs no sin.

4:22 Yadri Chaa Laabha Santush Taha
Dvan Dvaa Teeto Vimat Saraha
Samas Sid Dhaava Siddhau Cha
Kritvaa Pina Nibadh Yatey

Contented with whatever comes on its own accord, free from a pair of opposites, devoid of envy of others, while performing is equipoised in success and failure, is never affected.

5:19   Ihai Vatair Jitas Sarga Ha
        Yeshaan Saamyey Stitam Manaha
        Nir Dosham Hi Saman Brahma
        Tasmaad Brahmani Tey Stitaa Haa

Those whose minds are established in equality of vision conquer the cycle of birth and death in this very life. They possess the flawless qualities of God and are therefore seated in the Absolute Truth peacefully.

5:20   Na Prahris Shyet Priyam Praapya
        Nod Vijet Praapya Chaa Priyam
        Sthira Buddhira Sam Moodaha
        Brahma Vid Brahmanis Sthita Ha

Established in God, having a firm understanding of divine knowledge and not hampered by delusion, they neither rejoice in getting something pleasant nor grieve on experiencing the unpleasant.

ABOUT THE AUTHOR

Suresh Srinivasan brings with him over 42 years of rich corporate experience, comprising 21 years in Sales and another 21 years in Learning and Development. He is currently the Co-founder and Director of Potentia Growth Technologies Pvt. Ltd.

Driven by his life's purpose—"making people realize that life is simple"—he has positively impacted the lives of over 1,13,478 participants globally through his flagship program, Stop Look Go Enthusiastic.

Motivated by this mission, he authored a book that draws leadership lessons from the Srimad Bhagavad Geetaa, aiming to inspire young professionals, aspiring leaders, and seasoned executives on their leadership journey.

In 2023, he successfully completed the prestigious program titled "Understanding Bhagavad Gita: A Journey Towards Leadership Excellence" from IIM Ahmedabad.

To know more or read professional recommendations, visit his LinkedIn profile:

https://www.linkedin.com/in/suresh-srinivasan/